HISTORIC FIGURES
in the
BUCKINGHAMSHIRE
LANDSCAPE

by

John Houghton

All royalties to
The Bletchley Park Trust

First published October 1997
by
The Book Castle
12 Church Street
Dunstable
Bedfordshire LU5 4RU

ISBN 1 871199 63 8

Front Cover and frontispiece: The Vale of Aylesbury

Computer typeset by Keyword, Aldbury, Hertfordshire.
Printed by Antony Rowe Ltd., Chippenham, Wiltshire.

CONTENTS

Page

Chapter

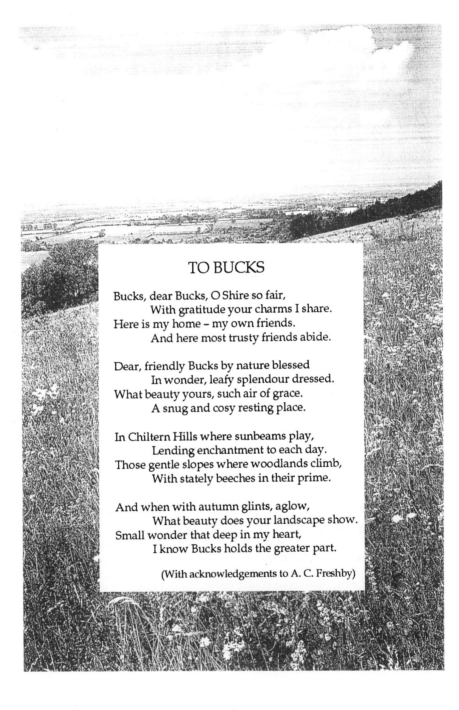

TO BUCKS

Bucks, dear Bucks, O Shire so fair,
    With gratitude your charms I share.
Here is my home – my own friends.
    And here most trusty friends abide.

Dear, friendly Bucks by nature blessed
    In wonder, leafy splendour dressed.
What beauty yours, such air of grace.
    A snug and cosy resting place.

In Chiltern Hills where sunbeams play,
    Lending enchantment to each day.
Those gentle slopes where woodlands climb,
    With stately beeches in their prime.

And when with autumn glints, aglow,
    What beauty does your landscape show.
Small wonder that deep in my heart,
    I know Bucks holds the greater part.

(With acknowledgements to A. C. Freshby)

FOREWORD
by
Sir Philip Duncombe Bt DL
Vice-Chairman, Bletchley Park Trust

John Houghton has assembled a great collection of interesting and intriguing people from the County, and his thorough research provides a fascinating record for generations to come.

My family has lived at Great Brickhill since the 16th Century, and I have had to admit a close association with the Chapter on Plotters as one of my ancestors was Everard Digby of Gayhurst. My father, who served in the Royal Bucks Hussars (but did not take part in the famous cavalry charge at El Mughar), was christened Everard, and my second name is Digby, so the reminder stays with us.

I can claim connections with another more honourable Chapter, i.e. Men at Arms. I have the privilege of following in the footsteps of three of Buckinghamshire's Gentlemen at Arms – Major Sir Henry Aubrey-Fletcher and Brigadier Sir Henry Floyd (both former Lord Lieutenants), and Brigadier John Cheney (the last Chief Constable of the County's Police Force before Thames Valley Police was formed), by serving in Her Majesty's Body Guard of the Honourable Corps of Gentlemen at Arms for the last eighteen years.

I must refer to the Wing Airport Resistance Association (WARA) formed to fight the proposals for siting the Third London Airport at Cublington. An historic local figure emerges as the leader of this amazingly successful campaign; he is Sir Desmond Fennell of Winslow, who was recently incapacitated by a stroke shortly after becoming a High Court Judge. His leadership and most able organisation have been recorded in other publications, and resistance organisations from other countries (including Japan) have visited Buckinghamshire to study the successful tactics which were adopted.

I hope very much that by the time this book is published the future of Bletchley Park will be assured, not only as a fitting memorial to those who worked there during World War II and to reproduce the atmosphere of ULTRA, but also to show future generations the evolution of the computer in telecommunication and information technology. My Chairman and fellow Trustees are very grateful to John Houghton for so generously donating the Royalties from this book to the Bletchley Park Trust.

Philip Duncombe

ABOUT THE AUTHOR

John Houghton was born in Sussex in 1916. From 1939 to 1942 he was Curate at Wolverton. From 1942 to 1974 he served in Central Africa as a Priest. In 1974 he returned to England and settled in Bletchley, retiring in 1983.

Also by John Houghton:

Borrowed Time Extended
Tales from Milton Keynes
Murders & Mysteries, People & Plots
Eccentrics & Villains, Hauntings & Heroes
Myths & Witches, Puzzles & Politics
Manors & Mayhem, Paupers and Parsons

PHOTOGRAPHS with the initials NK are by Norman Kent. Those with the initials JH are by the author

PREFACE

'God gives all men all earth to love,
But since man's heart is small,
Ordains for each one spot shall prove
Beloved over All'.

Rudyard Kipling wrote those words in praise of Sussex. He wasn't born there – he was born in Bombay.

Many of the 100 'figures in a Buckinghamshire landscape' recorded in this book would happily borrow Kipling's verse and adapt its last line. It would then continue:

'Each to his choice and I rejoice
The lot has fallen to me
In a fair ground – in a fair ground,
BUCKINGHAMSHIRE for me.'

For some of the 100 notables in this book, Bucks is where they found fame and fortune; or lost their fortune and even their lives. Poetic genius flourished for some, while others built great houses, still part of our national heritage.

Heroic deeds and eccentricity are here. And so, too, are ordinary folk who sometimes did extraordinary things.

And in a final chapter we meet the 12,000 extraordinary 'figures in a Buckinghamshire landscape' who were the Code Breakers of Bletchley Park.

THE ROYALTIES ON THIS BOOK WILL GO TO THE BLETCHLEY PARK TRUST, TO ASSIST ITS EFFORTS TO MAKE OF BLETCHLEY PARK A WORTHY TRIBUTE TO THEM AND TO PRESERVE A VERY SIGNIFICANT PART OF OUR NATIONAL HERITAGE.

ILLUSTRATIONS

Chapter 1

Historic Figures in the Buckinghamshire Landscape

The Brickhills, the Chilterns, the Vale of Aylesbury and Burnham Beeches – these are important components in the attractive landscape of Buckinghamshire. It is a county of much beauty and rural charm. And it is small. It measures under fifty miles from north to south, and a mere twenty miles from east to west. That makes it only 31st in county size in England. Its population, the 27th in England, occupies a modest 750 square miles.

John Betjeman wrote of the Vale of Aylesbury: 'It is real country where agriculture is a primary occupation, where the same families have lived for generations, where the farms and villages are the gradual growth of centuries, the new blending comfortably with the old'.

Sir Arthur Bryant wrote of: 'the beauty of the Vale . . . that chequered landscape of soft greens and browns, reflected clouds and blue horizons, unsurpassed anywhere in England'.

To complete the trio of enthusiasts, there is A. G. MacDonell who, in 'England, their England', wrote of: 'the loveliest of English names, the Vale of Aylesbury. Pasture and hedge, mile after mile, grey-green and brown and russet and silver, where little rivers tangle themselves among reeds and trodden watering-pools'.

Truth to tell, the County hardly possesses a river of any size. Streams and brooks it has, but no great river. It is true that the Great Ouse wanders for a few miles through the north-west corner of Bucks on its leisurely way to Bedfordshire. For the rest, Bucks is bounded, roughly speaking, by the Valleys of the Thames, the Colne and the Great Ouse.

But if rivers are not significant in Bucks, roads always have been. The county is crossed by a number of them, and their story goes back well into pre-Roman times.

The Ridgeway, running along the top of chalk downland ridges, crosses into Bucks near Goring on the Thames, traverses the Chiltern Hills, and leaves Bucks for Herts over Pitstone Hill near Ivinghoe Beacon. For centuries men walked the Ridgeway with their sheep and cattle.

The Icknield Way derives its name from the Iceni, the Celtic tribe who inhabited East Anglia. Over time, a sort of two-way traffic developed along the Ridgeway/Icknield Way – corn and cattle from the east and mineral wealth from the west. Such roads were not planned or designed – they just happened. They kept sensibly to the ridges and avoided the mud and swamps of lower ground.

Other ancient roads to cross Bucks were Akeman Street and Fosse Way. The former enters Bucks at Tring, passes Aylesbury, and leaves the county on the Bicester Road. The latter ran from Lincoln down to Cornwall and a branch of it ran through Water Stratford and Stony Stratford.

Some of these ancient roads were made use of by the Romans, whose own approach to roads and their making was quite different. Theirs were planned and precise, key parts of their strategy to control and administer the country they had invaded. And perhaps the greatest of their roads was the Watling Street which ran from London to Carlisle and passed through North Bucks on its way. It thus constituted a great north-west diagonal across England. Centuries later the pattern was repeated, as, first, Canals, then Railways, and finally the M1 all followed along that north-west diagonal, and all crossing North Bucks on their way.

What's in a Name?

We know the county as Buckinghamshire, but not until 1062 do we find it called by that name. Yet shires had been formed as early as the 9th century. It was King Alfred (840–901) who divided the country into Counties and Hundreds. Till then the country comprised only parishes. Alfred grouped parishes into Hundreds and then put adjoining Hundreds into Shires or Counties.

But Alfred did more than that. With great courage and skill he faced the Danes who held sway over so much of England. By the Treaty of Wedmore (871) he secured that the Danelaw would extend no further south than a line which he defined as follows:

> 'Let the bounds of our Dominion stretch to the River Thames and from thence to the Water of Lea, and then straight into Bedford, and finally, along by the River Ouse, let them end at Watling Street.

Within 'the bounds of our Dominion', the County of Buckinghamshire was thus safe within the Kingdom of Mercia. But its continuing safety had to be fought for. Alfred's son, Edward the Elder, had to do battle for it. Key to its defence were the strongholds of Bedford and Buckingham. And it is from the second of these that our county name derives.

But the etymology of the name 'Buckingham' is disputed. Popular opinion had it that it derives from the Anglo-Saxon 'Bucken', or 'Bucca', meaning beech tree. And certainly beech forests extended southwards from the Chilterns. Camden went along with that notion.

But for Spelman 'Buceen' meant bucks or deer. And Browne Willis agreed with him. But Lysons, in 'Magna Britannia', was more fanciful. For him, this was 'Bockland', in contradistinction to 'Folkland'.

But that is not all. The 'passing of the buck' goes on! For Sheahan, Buckingham derives its name from the Anglo-Saxons who owned it – the Buckings or Bockings. And Roscoe accepted that idea. He wrote:

'Buckingham owes its name directly to an Anglo-Saxon Thane, one Buck or Bock, whose heirs and dependents would be the Bockings, ("ing" being the Anglo-Saxon patronymic suffix). Hence the name of their settlement, "Buck-ing-ham", home of the family of Bock or Buck.'

So, if Roscoe is right, that Thane long ago, Buck or Bock,

takes his place alongside another Thane, Blecca, whose 'ley' or clearing in the Whaddon forest gave us 'Blecca's ley', Bletchley, a mere ten miles from 'Buck's ham', Buckingham.

Buckinghamia

On the very first true map of Bucks, made by the incredible Christopher Saxton in 1579, the county is called Buckinghamia. Christopher Saxton produced the first printed Atlas of the English and Welsh counties, the fruit of his labours in the 1570s. When it was published in 1579 it was the first uniform national Atlas to appear for any country.

Queen Elizabeth, through Burghley, commissioned the great work. Saxton surveyed every single English and Welsh county, on fifty-four maps. They are of astonishing accuracy and great beauty. Yet it was all accomplished in the space of five summer seasons – a feat surely on a par with the unbelievable speed with which the Domesday Survey had been carried out five hundred years before in one short year.

The need for Saxton's maps was in large measure due to the threat from Spain. The defence of the realm called for such maps. And the making of those maps relied heavily on the existence of the chain of beacons across the countryside. A Letter from the Privy Council made the point:

> 'An open Letter to all Justices of peace mayours and others within the several Shieres . . . That where the bearer hereof Christofer Saxton is appointed by her Maiestie under her signe and signet to set forth and describe Coates (Cartes) . . . That the said Justices shalbe aiding and assisting unto him to see him conducted unto any towre Castle highe place or hill to view that countrey, and that he may be accompanied with 2 or 3 honest men such as do best know the countrey for the better accomplishment of that service . . .'.

So in due course Saxton arrived in Bucks to do his survey. And it would be on Ivinghoe Beacon that he would chiefly rely, for Ivinghoe Beacon, at a height of some 820 feet, was a most

John Speed's Map of Bucks.

notable link in the great chain of beacons. From its commanding height Saxton could survey a panorama of outstretching country extending from the wooded borders of Bedfordshire, across the Vale of Aylesbury, to the distant heights of Ashenden and Brill. He would also have mounted Combe Hill and Aston Hill, and revelled in their splendid views, as we can still do today.

Together with his Maps, Saxton also included an Index for each, giving essential data. For 'Buckinghamia' he supplies these details:

> No cities; No Bishoprics; 11 Market Towns;
> No Castles; 185 Parishes; 2 Rivers; 14 Bridges;
> No Chases; No Forests; 15 Parks.

Such was the Bucks landscape as Saxton saw it in the 1570s. He was followed later by Morden (1695), Cary (1787) and Moule (1848), all of whom made maps of our county. But pride of place belongs to Christopher Saxton (1570), 'the father of English cartography'.

County Capital

When Alfred first created shires in 888, Buckingham became the county town of the shire to which it gave its name. It remained as such till the reign of Henry VIII. By then its fortunes had declined. The Assizes were removed to Aylesbury and for a while Buckingham was listed as one of the thirty-six most impoverished towns in England. Finally Henry VIII decreed that Aylesbury should be the County Town.

This made geographical sense. Six main roads converge on Aylesbury and the town has a history going back to the 6th century, when it was one of the strongest British fortresses. It fell to the Saxons in 571.

In 1204 King John presented Aylesbury to the Earl of Essex. Later it became the property of Thomas Bullen, the father of Anne Boleyn who was known as 'the fair maid of Aylesbury'. She caught the eye of Henry VIII with the fatal result of which all the world knows.

Burnham Beeches

Nowhere else in England are there beech woods so extensive or so fine as those at Burnham. By September's end each year they present their glorious spectacle of yellow, red and bronze foliage. This is the area of three Hundreds – Stoke, Desborough and Burnham. It is an area where in time past bands of lawless men gathered. They earned such notoriety that a special functionary was appointed to deal with the scandal and menace which they represented. From that unlikely background, the title of 'Steward of the Chiltern Hundreds' has passed into our language to describe a parliamentary oddity.

No member of the House of Commons is allowed to resign his or her seat during the course of a Parliament. But equally no member is allowed to occupy any 'office of profit' belonging to the crown. Since the 18th century these two restrictions have been neatly combined. A member wishing to resign a seat applies to become Steward of the Chiltern Hundreds. The office once carried a salary from the crown but is now defunct. So the member who applies for the Stewardship has no duties and is paid nothing. He or she must relinquish the seat in Parliament. And then promptly also resign the Stewardship so as to make it available for another applicant!

North Buckinghamshire

The contrasts of landscapes within so small a county as Bucks are very marked. North and South Bucks are divided by the Chiltern Hills. To the south of the Chilterns lies the Burnham Plateau with its wealth of beech and other trees. To their north lies the Vale of Aylesbury and the Valley of the Ouse.

North Bucks is an area of mixed agriculture – large fields and first-rate farming. It is an area of low heights, woods and copses, farmlands and pleasant villages. On the border between Bucks and Beds lie The Brickhills, and their three villages – Bow, Little, and Great. There are the small, old and attractive towns also – Olney, Stony Stratford, Buckingham and Winslow. And great houses too, with their parks – Gayhurst, Tyringham, Chicheley, Claydon, Stowe, Waddesdon, Mentmore, Ascott.

And it is here also that the new city of Milton Keynes has been created. Aptly, it was our own North Bucks poet, Cowper, who penned the line: 'God made the country; man made the town'.

Conceived in the 1960s, Milton Keynes was built in the years that followed. It links three established towns, Bletchley, Stony Stratford and Wolverton and takes in some twenty villages and smaller settlements, some going back to medieval and Norman times. One of these, the tiny village of Milton Keynes, gives its name to the new metropolis. By the year 2000 'MK's' population will be about 200,000. The city is spacious and is studded with woods, lakes and recreational parks.

Tiny though it is, the County of Bucks has figured largely in every chapter of our national history. It is the creation of successive waves of peoples who have carried the story forward from the Iron Age, the Romans and Saxons and Normans, the Elizabethans and on into modern times.

Because of its nearness to London, it has attracted statesmen and politicians, men of letters, men of wealth, artists, planners and builders – and quite a few eccentrics as well! And it has always had its own native sons, born and bred in the County of Bucks.

These are the historic figures in the Landscape sketched above. What follows are the stories of over a hundred of them. AND IN A FINAL CHAPTER A FURTHER 12,000 OF THEM! – THE CODE BREAKERS OF BLETCHLEY PARK.

Chapter 2

Men at Arms

Those who are old enough remember how, after the fall of France in World War II, Hitler spent many months assembling a huge number of 'invasion barges' on the coasts of France and Belgium in preparation for the invasion of England. Mercifully, that invasion, code-named 'Operation Sea Lion', never took place.

Almost exactly 1,000 years before that, William, Duke of Normandy, assembled *his* 'invasion barges' on that same coast for *his* invasion of England. And that invasion, as every schoolboy knows, did take place. And, it could be added, William had a lot more justification for his invasion than did Hitler. After all, he had connections with King Edward the Confessor, and claimed to have been promised the English throne by him.

Just another 1,000 years before William's successful invasion of England, the Romans made their successful invasion – from those same coasts, across the same narrow waters of the English Channel.

Of the 'men at arms' on the English side facing that Roman invasion we have very little detail. Caesar invaded twice, in 55 and 54 BC. But these were raids rather than an invasion proper which did not take place until AD43.

British resistance was led by Caractacus who was the son of Cunobelin, or Cymbaline as Shakespeare called him in his play. Within four years the Romans had made the Fosse Way which ran from Devon to Lincoln and passed through Bucks *en route*. In Bucks too lie Great and Little Kimble – perhaps the oldest village name in the county. Some have said that the name Kimble is derived from Cymbeline, and that there is a connection to be traced between Chenebelle (the Domesday name for Kimble) and Cunobeline (the alternative name of Cunobelin or Cymbeline). More than that, some have said that Cunobelinus, who was the king or chieftain of the Catevellauni, acquitted himself so well against the Romans that he was styled Rex Brittanicus and was able to mint his own coins bearing that title.

And to complete the picture, some have said that his castle or residence were on the hilltop at Great Kimble, the Hill being popularly known as Cymbeline's Mount. It would be quite splendid if that were so! Certainly Cymbeline's Mount does exist, and it stands virtually in the grounds of Chequers Court, the country home of the British Prime Minister. How stirring to think that successive Prime Ministers, strolling in the beautiful grounds at Chequers, can look upon the scene of triumph of a great British hero king who successfully withstood the Roman invaders 2,000 years ago and ruled as Rex Brittanicus!

Cymbeline's Mount from Ellesborough. (JH)

Alas, reality dismisses the myth. Cunobelinus, or Cymbeline, did exist, and he was the Chief of the Catevellauni. But his headquarters were at Colchester, not at Chequers, and he didn't defeat the Romans. Cymbeline's Mount no doubt was a hill fort, but it was just one of several such in the Chilterns.

When it came, 1,000 years later to William's invasion, a great many people contributed to the fleet of 'invasion barges' he needed. Several of them were kinsmen to William, some of them were bishops, and three of them have especial relevance in Bucks history. They were: Geoffrey, Bishop of Coutances, Odo, Bishop of Bayeux, and Walter Giffard. All were awarded a great many Saxon Manors in widely scattered parts of the country. But for our purposes it is the Manors in Bucks which matter. To Geoffrey, Bishop of Coutances, were awarded eighteen of these, including Water Eaton and Simpson. To Odo, Bishop of Bayeux and half-brother to the Conqueror himself were given twenty-six manors in North Bucks. And to Walter Giffard, also a kinsman of the Conqueror, were awarded forty-eight Manors. They take up five columns in the Domesday Book, and amounted to a sixth of the whole county of Bucks. And it was soon a case of 'to him that has much, shall even more be given'. This came about because when William I died, he was succeeded by his second son, Rufus, who became William II, while his first-born son, Robert, was left with the Dukedom of Normandy. Robert was furious at this and wanted the English throne. To try to secure it he raised a rebellion, and in this he was supported by both Bishop Geoffrey and Bishop Odo. The rebellion failed and both bishops were stripped of their Manors. Those Manors were then awarded to Walter Giffard.

These three, then, were among the Men at Arms at the Conquest and during its aftermath. We may wonder that two of these Men at Arms were also Men of the Cloth, yet so it was. And as for Walter Giffard, his family was destined to hold sway in Bucks for the next hundred years or more.

One other Man at Arms at the Conquest was a specialist. His name was Lovett and he was William the Conqueror's Master of Wolfhounds! His family was given the Manor of Soulbury, Liscombe Park, and there have been Lovetts at Soulbury for well over six hundred years. There are memorials to them in Soulbury Church, including one by Grinling Gibbons. The celebrated sculptor is most famous for his wood carving, but he also worked in marble. The example of his work in Soulbury Church shows his skill in both mediums. It comprises an urn with cherubs, carved in marble, surmounted by a wood carving, appropriately, of a black wolf.

❖ ❖ ❖ ❖ ❖

We should next pick up the matter of Men at Arms and their place in Bucks history some four centuries later – in the Wars of the Roses. The Plantagenet dynasty was split in rivalry. One faction was led by Edmund, Duke of York – the White Rose. The other was led by his brother, John of Gaunt, Duke of Lancaster – the Red Rose. Both were sons of Edward III.

The Red and White Rose emblems were not the only floral badges. There was a third – the Broom. The royal dynasty in England from Henry II to Richard III is known by historians as Plantagenet. This is because Henry II's father, Geoffrey of Anjou, sported a sprig of broom as his badge, and, in Old French, broom is 'plante genet'.

The plantagenet dynasty split in rivalry into two factions. One, led by Edmund, Duke of York, adopted the White Rose; the other, led by John of Gaunt, Duke of Lancaster, adopted the Red Rose. These Dukes were brothers, sons of Edward III.

The rivalry between them led to thirty years of intermittent Civil War, to many murders, and to several shocking episodes of deceit and treachery. It is said that twelve royal princes perished, as well as some two hundred nobles and 100,000 ordinary folk.

In the turbulent 15th century every baron had what amounted to a private army. It might only be a modest handful of armed retainers. Or, where one individual held a large number of Manors, it could well amount to a force of over one thousand men at arms.

In the dynastic struggle between Red and White Roses, sides had to be taken, support pledged or withheld, and, sometimes promises reneged on and sides changed!

How did Bucks fare in this time of upheaval? Lord Grey de Ruthin, of Bletchley, supported the Red Rose of Lancaster. The Longuevilles of neighbouring Wolverton declared for the White Rose of York. So too did Humphrey Stafford of Little Brickhill. But see what happened on the eve of the Battle of Northampton! Edmund, Baron Grey, Lord of the Manors of Bletchley, Simpson and Great Brickhill, set off with all his men at arms to join the battle some twenty miles away at Northampton on the side of the Red Rose of Lancaster. But when he and they arrived, the Baron had changed his mind, and he declared himself for the Yorkist, White Rose, cause! This dramatic switch did not go unrewarded. Later, when the Lord Protector's son had become King Edward IV, Baron Edmund was named Lord Treasurer. And two years later, in 1465, he was created Earl of Kent.

When we come to the tragic events of the Civil War in the next century it is certain individual men at arms whose actions and experience engage out attention.

There was John Hampden, of Great Hampden, Buckinghamshire's greatest hero. He refused to pay the forced loan demanded by Charles I, and was sent to prison. Next he refused to pay the Ship Money Tax which the King wanted to extend to inland counties. He was one of the five MPs that Charles tried to seize in Parliament. He raised a County Regiment of Infantry for the Parliamentary Army. When the Civil War broke out he fought at the Battle of Chalgrave Field where he was wounded, dying later from that wound. He was described by one biographer as 'the most moderate, tactical,

John Hampden's Statue in Aylesbury.

Hampden House, Great Hampden. John Hampden is buried in the nearby Church.

urbane and single-minded of the leaders of the Long Parliament'. The circumstances of his times required that this urbane man should become a man at arms.

For Edmund Verney of Claydon the outbreak of the Civil War brought a crisis of conscience. His head told him that the King was in the wrong, but his heart told him that he must nevertheless support the King, whose Royal Standard Bearer he was. So it was a reluctant but courageous man at arms who stood his ground at the Battle of Edgehill in 1642, where the Royal Standard had to be hacked from his hand in the thick of battle, and his life was lost.

But if Edmund Verney of Claydon was wracked with doubt as to whether or not he should support the King, his neighbour and kinsman by marriage, Alexander Denton of nearby Hillesden, had no such doubts. The Dentons were wholeheartedly for the King. So much so that they set to work to fortify Hillesden, determined to make of it a Royalist stronghold in the depths of the Bucks landscape. The house, the church, and the park itself were all fortified and placed on a war footing. So the Lord of Hillesden and his dependants and tenants stood to their arms and awaited the onslaught.

There is an old saying: 'Do as you wish – and pay for it'. At Hillesden they knew what they wished – to make their part of Bucks safe for the King. And they paid for it. Out from the Parliamentary stronghold of Aylesbury came the Roundhead troops, led by Cromwell himself. They overthrew the Hillesden

Denton Tomb at Hillesden, damaged by Roundheads. (NK)

defences and set the great house on fire, reducing it to ruins. Sir Alexander Denton was taken prisoner and died, it is said, of a broken heart.

Earlier in the Civil War, indeed even before the war was technically begun by Charles raising his standard at Nottingham in 1642, the Lord of the Manor of Boughton, just outside Buckingham, made his decision. He was Sir Richard Minshull. He gathered together a small company of his retainers and dependants and, leaving their normal peace-time pursuits, they set off to join the King at Nottingham. They too were doing what they wished – and they paid for it. As would later happen to Hillesden, so now to Boughton Manor there came out from Aylesbury Parliamentary troops, and they laid Boughton Manor to waste. It was a pre-emptive strike, intended to discourage other landowners who might rally to the King's cause.

Another man at arms in the Civil War who had his own distinctive part to play was Robert Hammond. He was born in 1621 and rose to be a Colonel in Cromwell's army. In 1642, when the Civil War began, he was made Captain of Foot and fought at the siege of Tewkesbury in 1644. In 1645 he was made Commander of a Foot Regiment in the New Model Army and fought at the Battle of Naseby. Following that battle he took part in the storming of Bristol and Dartmouth. He saw action also at Torrington and captured Powderham Castle.

Hammond was a Presbyterian by conviction. But, despite having taken up arms against the King, he retained an instinctive sense of loyalty to the monarchy.

He was appointed Governor of the Isle of Wight and took up residence in Carisbrooke Castle there. King Charles escaped from Hampton Court in November 1647 and made his way to the Isle of Wight. This was an acute embarrassment to Hammond who was appalled to find himself the King's Jailor. He later explained: 'I knew not what course to take; but upon serious consideration . . . I resolved it my duty to the King, to the Parliament and kingdom to use the utmost of my endeavours to preserve his person'.

Hammond at first treated Charles with great deference and decorum, but Charles soon began to plot and try to escape. Eventually Hammond was ordered to deliver the King to London in 1648 and there the King was put on trial and was executed on January 30th 1649.

Hammond's connection with Bucks is two-fold. He had married a daughter of John Hampden and in 1653 he purchased the Manor of Willen. Cromwell appointed him as a Member of the Irish Council and Hammond went to Ireland to start work on the reorganisation of the Irish Judicial System. But in October 1654 he died in Ireland of a fever.

When the Monarchy was restored in 1660 the hunt was on for the regicides, who had signed the Death Warrant of Charles I. It might have been expected that the estates of the King's estwhile Jailor would be seized. But in fact they were not and Hammond's family were left in possession of Willen.

Two other men at arms with strong Bucks connections are commemorated by memorials in churches.

The first is William Ovitts of Winslow. He died, aged 87, on 20th November 1830 and was buried on the south side of Winslow Parish Church. In his youth he had enlisted in the Regiment of Light Dragoons which saw service on the continent in the Seven Years War (1756–63). The Regiment fought at the Battle of Freyburgh. The Hereditary Prince of Brunswick was captured by three French Dragoons. Young Ovitt witnessed the incident and galloped after them. Astonishingly, he killed all three Frenchmen, rescued the Prince and was himself wounded. Despite his wounds he brought the Prince back safely to the allied lines. The Prince, suitably grateful, gave young Ovitt a Purse of 100 guineas.

Other Officers in the Dragoons, so impressed by Ovitt's dash and bravery, wanted to recommend him for a Commission. But Ovitt declined – he thought his humble origins and lack of education made him unsuitable to be an Officer. When the Duke of Buckingham heard about this he announced that Ovitt should be paid an allowance of one shilling a day for the rest of his life. Ovitt lived till 1830, so he enjoyed that unusual pension for over sixty years. And his memory lives still in Winslow where he was buried.

The second individual man at arms commemorated in a Bucks church is Neil Archibald Primrose. His memorial is in Mentmore Church.

Mentmore Towers was built by Baron Mayer de Rothschild in the 1850s. It was inherited by his daughter Hannah, who in 1878 married Archibald Primrose, fifth Earl of Rosebery. It is their son, Neil James Archibald Primrose who is commemorated in Mentmore Church in these words:

To the beloved memory of
Captain the Right Hon
Neil James
Archibald Primrose
MP for Wisbech and MC
Born at Dalmeny, Dec.14 1882
And killed Nov 15 1917
While leading a Charge
Of the Royal Bucks Hussars
at the hill of Gezer
Near which at Ramleh
he lies buried.
This Tablet is erected by his
Proud and sorrowful Father.

Now he is dead
Far hence to lie
In the lorn Syrian Town
And in his grave
with shining eyes
The Syrian Stars look down.

It is said that this Cavalry Charge made in 1917 at El Mughar in Palestine by the Royal Bucks Hussars was the last Cavalry Charge ever made by the British Army.

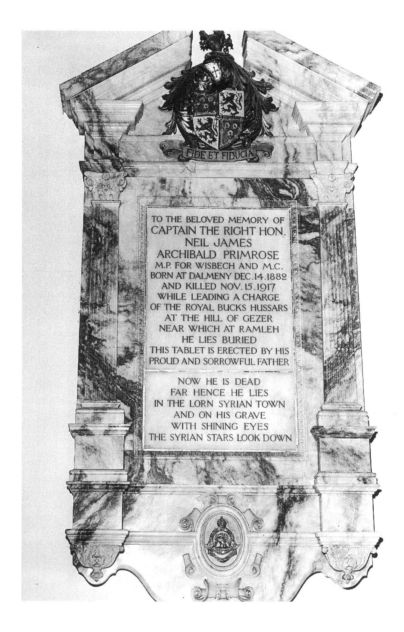

Capt. Primrose Memorial in Mentmore Church. (NK)

Another Man at Arms of Buckinghamshire relevance, also of World War I vintage, was John French. He was born in Kent in 1852 and joined the Army in 1874, after a very brief spell in the Navy. He saw service in the Sudan and in South Africa.

As a young lieutenant he married into the well-known Buckinghamshire family of Richard Selby-Lowndes. He and his young wife made their first married home in Bracknell House in Fenny Stratford. (Today the house is a Registry Office).

For the three years immediately preceding World War I Sir John French was Chief of Imperial General Staff. When war broke out in August 1914 he took command of the British Expeditionary Force in France. When General Haig succeeded him Sir John became Commander-in-Chief Home Forces in 1915, and finally became a Field Marshal.

He was raised to the peerage and took as his title: Lord French, 1st Earl of Ypres – an insensitive choice perhaps, given the great numbers who perished in and round Ypres. From 1918 to 1921 he was Lord Lieutenant of Ireland during the Anglo-Irish War.

In later years he separated from his wife and chose to live in France. His widow, Lady French, died in 1941 and is buried in Bletchley Churchyard.

Chapter 3

Men of State

*'There is something in the air of Bucks favourable
to political knowledge and vigour.'*

It was Benjamin Disraeli who said that. He was born in London
but brought up in Bucks at Bradenham. And he lived in Bucks
at his splendid house at Hughenden. He is one of six Prime
Ministers who came out of Bucks to hold that office (twice: 1860
and 1868–70).

> *'Politics have been the pride of Bucks. Her political
> position was achieved in the 18th century and lasted till
> politics passed out of the hands of the grandees and
> became popular and democratic. I claim for Bucks that
> she is the most famous of English counties in the field of
> politics during that period.'*

That was the Earl of Rosebery who, like Disraeli, came out
of Bucks (and his palatial seat at Mentmore Towers) to hold the
office of Prime Minister (1894–95).

As well as Disraeli and Rosebery, other Prime Ministers to
come out of Bucks to Westminster were:

> George Temple, PM 1763–65
> William Pitt, PM 1766–67
> Pitt the Younger, PM 1783–1801 and 1804–1806
> William Grenville, PM 1806–1807

So, in the forty-four years from 1763 to 1807 four Prime
Ministers, all related by blood or by marriage, emerged from
that group often referred to as the 'Cobham Cousins' whose
powerbase was Stowe. And, with Disraeli and Rosebery

coming as Prime Ministers later, it means that in the 140 years between 1763 and 1895 Bucks provided no less than six Prime Ministers.

But before looking in greater details at these men of state, there are others we should notice in the centuries preceding them.

Walter Giffard

Actually there were three Walter Giffards. The first Walter Giffard, related to the Conqueror, was awarded more Manors than anybody else outside the Conqueror's immediate family. He was Lord of Longueville in Normandy and was virtually Commander of the Norman Army at the Battle of Hastings. It was not surprising, therefore, that this Man at Arms would be so rewarded, and made so very much a Man of State over large areas of Bucks.

The Giffard dynasty held sway in Bucks for just over a century till the male line ceased. The Walter Giffards II and III were both made Earls of Buckingham and both were involved in national affairs. Walter Giffard II was a witness to King Henry I's Charter of Liberties in 1101. Walter Giffard III was appointed Marshal of England. But after his death there were no more male Giffards to continue the line.

But if the Giffards were the first to take their title from the county, they were not the last. In 1377 Thomas Plantagenet, youngest son of Edward III, was created Earl of Buckingham. In that title he was succeeded by his son, Humphrey who in his turn was succeeded by his nephew. Two later descendents in this line bore the title, not of Earl of Buckingham but as Duke.

In ascending order, the five ranks of the peerage are: Baron, Viscount, Earl, Marquess, Duke. We meet all of them in this review of Men of State who have figured in Bucks history. In the time of the Stuarts there were the two Villiers. George Villiers well illustrates the progress a man of state could make. In 1616 he became Earl of Buckingham. In 1618 he became Marquis, and in 1623 Duke. He was a great favourite of Charles I but was enormously unpopular in the country at large. Hampden and others wanted to impeach him, and might have done so had not an assassin got in first. The Duke was murdered in Portsmouth.

His son George, the second Duke of Buckingham, supported Charles in the Civil War and fled to exile in France with the King's son. After the Restoration he was made a Privy Councillor, but in 1674 he was dismissed from office.

In 1713 John Sheffield was created Duke of Buckingham, but the title in this family became extinct on the death of his successor in 1735. And the next family whose members took the title of Buckingham were the Temples. Their family name was Grenville.

George Grenville, Earl Temple, was made Marquis of Buckingham in 1784. He was twice made Lord Lieutenant of Ireland. The Bucks/Ireland connection is one that has repeated itself three times over. The Marquis of Buckingham was sent as Lord Lieutenant of Ireland in the 18th century. But long before that, in the 16th century, Lord Grey de Wilton, Lord of the Manor of Whaddon in Bletchley, had also been sent to Ireland as Lord Deputy (see page 52). And Robert Hammond, Lord of the Manor of Willen, also served in Ireland.

And history repeated itself again in the 20th century. John French when a young Lieutenant married one of the eight daughters of Richard Selby – Lowndes. Their first married home was Bracknell House in Fenny Stratford, now a Registry Office. Then came World War I. John French rose to the highest rank in the British Army and became a Field Marshal. He was raised to the peerage as Lord French, 1st Earl of Ypres. And from 1918 to 1921 he was Viceroy of Ireland – the third notable with direct Bucks connections to hold such office.

The Reformation in England in the 16th century had both political and doctrinal overtones. At the heart of the matter was the dynastic problem of succession – Henry VIII's urgent and passionate desire for a son to succeed him. It led him to wed six wives, and only Jane Seymour, his third wife, bore him a son. But he was a sickly child and his mother died twelve days after giving him birth. When Henry VIII died in 1547 the sickly chid, by then ten years old, succeeded as Edward VI. He reigned, through a Protector, for six years, dying in 1553.

Who should succeed him? Speculation was rife. Should it be Mary, daughter of Catherine of Aragon, Henry's first wife? Or should it be Elizabeth, daughter of Anne Boleyn, Henry's second wife? The two were half-sisters to each other and to the young Edward VI who had just died. Many great landowners and Lords of Manors in Bucks were caught up in the great debate, some supporting Mary, others Elizabeth. Henry's divorces had pronounced both Mary and Elizabeth to be bastards. So there were some who considered both to be ruled out of the succession.

An alternative existed, some thought, in the person of the young Lady Jane Grey. She was, after all, a granddaughter of Henry VII through a female line and was therefore of Tudor stock.

Of especial significance to some in Bucks was the fact that her name was Grey. William, 13th Baron Grey of Wilton and Water Hall, Bletchley, was a distant cousin. He had succeeded to the Bletchley estates in 1529 and had distinguished himself in the French and Scottish Wars. He was naturally a keen supporter of the plan to place Lady Jane Grey on the throne. Moreover, his young son, Arthur, was betrothed to Lady Jane Grey's eight year old sister, Mary!

So Baron Grey of Bletchley made plans to proclaim Jane as Queen in a great demonstration at Aylesbury. But he was forestalled. His neighbour, Sir William Dormer of Wing got in first and declared in favour of Mary Tudor.

Mary Tudor herself was not idle! She declared herself Queen in London and was supported by 1,000 men from Bucks, Northants and Oxford. She contrived to eliminate her half-sister Elizabeth by sending her as a virtual prisoner to Woodstock. Later, however, she thought it wiser to have Elizabeth in London where she could keep an eye on her. So Elizabeth was brought from Woodstock to the capital, spending a night in the Dormer's house, Ascott at Wing, *en route*.

The Grey faction had to abandon their support of Lady Jane, who herself had no desire to be Queen anyway. She and her young husband were sent to the Tower and there executed. But the ruthless Mary had not yet completed her revenge. She had the Duke of Northumberland executed for leading the Lady Jane faction. And what about William, Lord Grey of Bletchley? He too was seized and imprisoned. He escaped execution, and was even pardoned, but only at the expense of being attainted, with all his honours and estates forfeited. The young Arthur Grey's betrothal to Lady Mary was broken off and the little girl went back to her nursery.

So these were black days for the Greys in Bletchley. But all came right later. Mary only reigned for five years. She died in 1537 and was succeeded after all by her half-sister Elizabeth, who restored all William Grey's honours and estates in Bletchley.

But this recovery of the Grey fortunes in Bletchley proved to be short-lived. William Grey was entrusted with the defence of Guisnes in France where he was taken prisoner. A ransom of 24,000 crowns was demanded for his release. The result was that when he died in 1562 his estates were hopelessly crippled with debt. A commentator wrote of him:

> 'Not much regarded was this gallant spirit when alive, but much missed when he was dead . . . the beauty of worthy things is not in the face, but in the backside, endearing more by their departure than by their address.'

So, in the swings and roundabouts of history, Elizabeth came to the throne in the place of her half-sister Mary. In place of the daughter of Catherine of Aragon, the daughter of Anne Boleyn now ruled.

A second cousin to Elizabeth was Sir John Fortescue, 'Knight, Chancellor of the Exchequer and of the Duchy of Lancaster, Master of the Wardrobe and of the Privy Council'. Elizabeth thought very highly of him. When she appointed him Keeper of the Great Wardrobe she declared that she 'trusted him with both the ornaments of her soul and body.'

John Fortescue's Memorial in Little Horwood Church. (NK)

John Fortescue became MP for Bucks and served in Parliament for forty years. In 1565 he bought the Manor of Salden near the village of Mursely. There he built his palatial Salden Manor at a cost of £33,000, a sum perhaps approaching a million in today's money. There he entertained Elizabeth more than once, and also her successor, James I. He came to Salden in the very first year of his reign, in 1603, and created twenty-two new Knights at a ceremony in the Great (150 feet long) Hall on the first floor of the palatial house.

The magnificence of Salden Manor came to an abrupt end after the Civil War. Fortescue's support of the king led to the sequestration of some of the Fortescue estates and the family finances were left in a parlous state. The Fortescue title became extinct finally in 1729. In 1738 the melancholy demolition of the great Salden Manor began. Today only a farmhouse marks its site.

Another man who built a new mansion in Bucks and in it entertained Queen Elizabeth was Sir Henry Lee (1539–1610). The Lees of Quarrendon were an ancient Bucks family. Sir Henry Lee was a Knight of the Garter and was the Queen's Champion. His family was prominent in the Vale of Aylesbury and Sir Henry founded the Aylesbury Free School. The Lee monument in Aylesbury Parish Church commemorates them not only by the wording of its inscription, but also in the touching ceremony, which still continues, that on a certain day each year a fresh red flower is placed upon the monument.

Twentieth century descendants of the Lee family were Lord and Lady Lee of Fareham. In the years before World War I they were searching for a suitable cottage in the Vale of Aylesbury. In the course of that search they came across an Elizabethan house near Ellesborough called Chequers. It was in a somewhat forlorn and neglected condition, but the Lees could see its possibilities. They determined to make its restoration their hobby. Their restoration was both effectively and sensitively done.

Then World War I broke out. The Lees turned the restored house into a Convalescent Hospital which they staffed and equipped at their own expense. The War ended. And it was then that Lord and Lady Lee knew what they wanted to do with the fine house which they had restored with such care. They would give it to the nation as a Thanksgiving for England's deliverance. And they wished the house to be 'a place of rest and recreation for Prime Ministers for ever'.

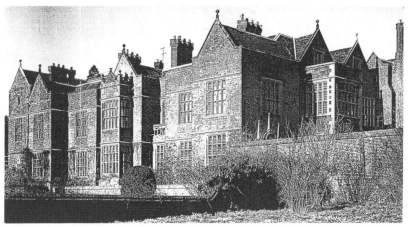

Chequers, country home for the Prime Minister.

In his Deed of Statement handing Chequers to the nation the far-seeing Lord Lee wrote in his Preface:

> *'It is not possible to foresee or foretell from what classes or conditions of life the future wielders of power in this country will be drawn. Some may be, as in the past, men of wealth and famous descent; some may belong to the world of trade and business; others may spring from the ranks of manual toilers. To none of these in the midst of their strenuous and responsible labours could the spirit and anodyne of Chequers do anything but good. In the city-bred man especially, the periodic contact with the most typical rural life would create and preserve a just sense of proportion between the claims of town and country. To the revolutionary statesman the antiquity and calm tenacity of Chequers and its annals might suggest some saving virtues in the continuity of English*

37

*history and exercise a check upon too hasty upheavals,
whilst even the most reactionary could scarcely be
insensible to the spirit of human freedom which permeates
the countryside of Hampden, Burke and Milton.'*

The first Prime Minister officially to use Chequers was
Lloyd George in 1921, and every Prime Minister since has used
Chequers. So the fine house has seen a succession, not only of
Prime Ministers, but also of many internationally-famous
people and world leaders who have been entertained there by
the Premier.

As well as presenting Chequers to the nation, Lord and
Lady Lee also donated Combe Hill to the National Trust in
1918. Combe Hill, at 825 feet, is the highest point in the
Chilterns. From Combe Hill there is the finest view of
Cymbeline's Mount which stands within the grounds of
Chequers. (See also page 18.)

How right Lord Lee was to write in his Preface about 'the
antiquity of Chequers'. Its ownership can be traced through a
long line of possessors for seven hundred years. There was
Elias de Scaccariis in the 12th century. He was also known as
Elias Chakers, which would seem to explain the origin of the
name Chequers. Lipscombe however thought the name derives
from Exchequer. He pointed out that the Exchequer was not
originally established at Westminster, but was itinerant,
accompanying the King's Court on each major royal progress.
But that was found to be inconvenient and so, by the Great
Charter of Henry III it was decreed that the Exchequer should
be permanently established at Westminster.

Roscoe, in his book 'Buckinghamshire' dismisses the idea that
even in its itinerant days the Exchequer could ever have been at
Chequers. But he is ready to admit that the property might have
belonged to an officer of the Exchequer. So perhaps Elias de
Scaccariis, popularly known as Elias Chakers was that man.

Chequers Court passed from father to son from Elias
Chakers until about the middle of the 13th century, when the
male line became extinct. The property then passed through a
daughter, Catherine, to William de Alta Ripa whom she

married. The name Alta Ripa became anglicized to Hawtrey. When the male line ceased in the Hawtrey ownership Chequers passed through marriage to the Russells.

In the 17th century another very well-known name comes into the story. Frances, the youngest daughter of Oliver Cromwell married Sir John Russell. Because of this connection several portraits of Oliver Cromwell came to Chequers and are there still. Other Cromwell memorabilia at Chequers include swords which belonged to the Protector and his Death Mask. Chequers remained in the possession of the Cromwell/Russell family right up to the beginning of the twentieth century when, as already related, it was acquired by Lord and Lady Lee who presented it to the nation.

If Chequers is unique as being the country home of the Prime Minister of the day, there is another great Bucks house which, nearly two centuries ago also had prime-ministerial connections four times over. That house was Stowe.

The Powerhouse of Stowe
The group of politicians who gathered at Stowe provided no less than four Prime Ministers within the space of forty years. These were 'the Cobham Cousins', as Lord Rosebery described them, the Grenvilles, Lyttletons and Pitts. Sir Frank Markham coined an apt phrase when he spoke of 'The Powerhouse of Stowe'.

Hester Temple, the wife of Richard Grenville, was a remarkable woman. She became a great political hostess and set the pattern for the political gatherings for which Stowe became famous. Her son, George, became Prime Minister in 1763. Her daughter, Hester, married in 1764 a young politician named William Pitt. Later, as Earl of Chatham, he too became Prime Minister in 1766.

Of the next generation, the second son of Hester and William Pitt, always known as Pitt the Younger, became Prime Minister not once but twice – in 1783 and in 1804. His first term as Prime Minister was at the astonishing age of twenty-four.

Stowe, an 18th century powerhouse. (JH)

And his cousin, William Grenville, also became Prime Minister in 1806.

Four Prime Ministers, then, all related by blood or marriage, emerged from that group whose power base was Stowe. It is instructive to see the historical context in which they were called upon to exercise their premierships.

In 1763, when George Grenville became PM, the Peace of Paris ended The Seven Years' War. The successful revolt of the American Colonies took place. When the elder Pitt was PM there was chaos in India and Clive left that country. During the premiership of the Younger Pitt, George III went mad; the French Revolution began; Louis XVI was executed; Napoleon became Commander in Chief and proceeded to win battles in Europe, in Egypt and in Palestine; the Act of Union of Great Britain and Ireland came into force in 1801.

In the second administration of Pitt the Younger (1804–06) Napoleon continued his string of victories and was crowned King of Italy. The British occupied the Cape of Good Hope. Joseph Bonaparte was named King of Naples. Louis Bonaparte was named King of Holland. The Holy Roman Empire was officially declared at an end.

Added to these international events and crises, at home there was the great Wilkes controversy, and the Trial of Warren Hastings. Stirring times, then, both at home and abroad.

After Grenville's premiership ended in 1807 the spotlight was on Stowe no longer – the great 'Powerhouse of Stowe' was no longer the engine of national government.

The next Man of State from Bucks to come to prominence was:

Benjamin Disraeli (1804–1881).

Of Jewish stock, his father nevertheless had him baptised in the Church of England in 1817 when young Benjamin was thirteen years old. His father was Isaac Disraeli, an English man of letters, whose home was the Manor House at Bradenham. It was here that the young Disraeli first learned to love the county of Bucks. After his father died in 1848 Benjamin Disraeli purchased Hughenden and made it his home for the rest of his life. At Hughenden he wrote all his novels (15 of them) and at Hughenden he delighted to play the role of landowner and Lord of the Manor. (For Disraeli the Man of Letters see page 55.)

Hughenden, Disraeli's home. (JH)

His first four attempts to enter Parliament were a failure, but he was successful in 1837, becoming MP for Maidstone. His maiden speech was a disaster, and amid the jeers and laughter of the House he sat down with the memorable words: 'Though I sit down now the time will come when you will hear me'.

In due time he became Chancellor of the Exchequer (1852) but his party was defeated in the election and the Tory Party went into Opposition, while Gladstone and the Liberals formed the Government. It was seven years before the Liberals were defeated and the Tories returned to power. Disraeli again became Chancellor of the Exchequer (1866). In February 1868 he succeeded Lord Derby as PM but his administration lasted only a few months. He was back in power again as PM in 1874. In 1875 he made Britain half-owner of the Suez Canal, and in 1876 he conferred on Queen Victoria the new title of Empress of India. In that same year, 1876, as Earl of Beaconsfield, he was called to the Upper House.

Disraeli's diplomacy at the Congress of Berlin (1878) averted further conflict between Russia and Turkey and earned the admiration of Bismark who said of Disraeli: 'Der alte Jude, das ist ein mann'.

In 1880, the Tories were defeated at the polls and Disraeli felt he had had enough. He retired to Hughenden and his writing, and there in 1881 he died. The strange bond of affection between Queen Victoria and the extrovert Disraeli is reflected in the monument the Queen erected in Hughenden Church in his honour:

> 'To the dear and honoured memory of Benjamin Disraeli, Earl of Beaconsfield, this memorial is placed by his grateful and affectionate Sovereign and friend, Victoria, R.I. "Kings love him that speaketh right" Proverbs xvi.13. Feb.27th, 1982.'

As the 19th century ended it brought the sixth and last Prime Minister to come out of Bucks to Westminster. He was:

Earl of Rosebery (1847–1929)
Archibald Philip Primrose was 5th Earl of Rosebery. In 1878 he

married Hannah, the daughter and heiress of Baron Mayer de Rothschild who had built the palatial Mentmore Towers. The wedding was the social event of the year. Disraeli gave the bride away and the distinguished guest list was headed by the Prince of Wales.

From 1881–83 Rosebery was Under-Secretary at the Home Office under Gladstone. In 1884 he became First Commissioner for Works. In 1886, and again from 1892 to 1894 he was Secretary for Foreign Affairs.

When Gladstone retired as Liberal PM in 1894 Rosebery succeeded him. But in the following year, 1895, the Liberals were defeated and went into Opposition. For about a year Rosebery remained Leader of the Liberal Opposition but resigned in 1896. Thereafter he was either Independent or Conservative.

In 1911 he was created Earl of Midlothian. Besides his politics, he was also a great and successful enthusiast for the Turf, winning the Derby three times. He was a writer too, publishing books on Pitt, Peel and Chatham, and on the last phase of Napoleon's career.

Chapter 4

Men of Letters

The catalogue of Men of Letters associated with Buckinghamshire is nothing if not impressive. Merely to list them is to make the point:

POETS: Milton, Gray, Cowper, Newton, Waller, Spenser, Shelley.

HISTORIANS AND DIARISTS: Lipscombe, Cole, Browne Willis.

NOVELISTS: Disraeli, Mary Shelley.

POLEMICISTS: Burke, Wilkes.

The extent to which Bucks can 'claim' these great literary figures varies from one to another. Some were Bucks born and bred and are buried in their native county. Others lived in Bucks for varying lengths of time. Many of the literary products which made these men great were actually penned in Bucks. And the greatest of them all is John Milton.

John Milton (1608–1674)
He is the greatest epic poet in the English language. He was born in 1608 in Cheapside and died in 1674, and was buried next to his father in Cripplegate. For five years, from 1632 to 1637, he lived with his parents at Horton in Northants, and his mother is buried there. While at Horton he wrote: 'Lycidas, Il Penseroso, L'Allegro', and the 'Masque Comus', which he wrote for production at Ludlow Castle.

His first period of residence in Bucks was brief but dramatic. It lasted only about a year. It was Chalfont St. Giles to which Milton came in 1665, fleeing from the Plague in London.

By then he was blind, but despite this handicap it was at Chalfont St. Giles that he completed Paradise Lost and began work on Paradise Regained.

His house at Chalfont St. Giles is the Milton Museum. In 1887 the house was almost lost. It was planned to demolish it brick by brick and to transport it for re-erection in America. Happily, the plan was scotched. A Public Subscription was raised to save the building. Queen Victoria personally donated £20, and Queen Elizabeth II visited the Museum in 1987 to celebrate the Centenary of the Appeal.

Quite apart from his poetic genius, Milton's life was quite astonishing in the range of his activities. He was, at different times, a would-be ordinand, a classical scholar, a traveller, a

John Milton's cottage, Chalfont St. Giles, now a Museum.

teacher, a polemicist and pamphleteer, and a Civil Servant. His matrimonial history was sometimes turbulent and he married three times. Divorce was the subject of four of his pamphlets. In religion he became a Puritan and in the Civil War he was an ardent anti-royalist and Parliamentarian. It followed therefore that at the Restoration of the Monarchy he was *persona non grata* and he feared imprisonment. In fact however he was left unmolested.

John Milton's life falls into three distinct phases. (So do his marriages!) The first phase saw Milton as the brilliant Cambridge scholar. His first poems were written at Cambridge. After Cambridge came visits to Italy and then he settled down with his parents at Horton. He regarded this period as the real preparation for his life's work as a poet. Earlier, while still at Cambridge, he had wondered whether he was destined for the ministry. That possibility dropped from his mind in the Horton period and all his concentration now was on the making of poetry – in Latin and Italian as well as in English. His studies included Greek as well as Latin, and he devoted time to a study of the Church Fathers. For two years also he undertook the tutoring or teaching of his nephews.

The second phase of his life lasted from 1640 to 1660. Significantly, this period covers the whole of the Civil War and of the Commonwealth under Cromwell. Throughout that time he wrote virtually no poetry at all. Instead, he was caught up in the great issues of the day – the struggle between King and Parliament, the issues of liberty and authority, and Puritanism. He became at once both a polemicist and a pamphleteer. His writings attacked episcopacy, advanced fierce arguments against censorship, and advocated the right to terminate marriage by divorce.

In 1649 he became Latin Secretary to Cromwell's Council. Foreign correspondence at that time was still conducted in Latin as being the only truly international language. After the King's execution, an event which shocked the countries of Europe, Milton, as Latin Secretary, became the chief apologist for the Commonwealth. He wrote a number of papers defending the execution, and the regicides who had signed the Death Warrant. His duties to the Council perforce ceased when the Monarchy was restored. For a while he went into hiding, fearing arrest and punishment for the prominent role he had played under Cromwell. But his fears were relieved by the passing of the Act of Indemnity and Oblivion. So, now no longer a quasi-Civil Servant, he resumed his life and work as a Poet. The third and last phase of his remarkable career had begun.

But before we turn to that last, so fruitful, third phase, which gave the world 'Paradise Lost', 'Paradise Regained' and 'Samson Agonistes', we should take note of the fact that from 1652 onwards his eyesight had deteriorated until he was finally blind. Besides this physical handicap there were also personal tragedies.

If his adult life fell clearly into three distinct phases, so too did his marriage. In 1642, at the age of thirty-four, he married a girl half his age. His young wife soon left him, and this is what prompted the writing of those four pamphlets advocating divorce. Later, the young wife returned and three daughters were born before she died in 1652.

The widower's blindness drew from him a stoical sonnet, 'On His Blindness', of which the opening line is: 'When I consider how my light is spent'. And the final line of the sonnet is even more familiar: 'They also serve who only stand and wait'.

In his final years his daughters, now young adults, became his eyes, taking turns in reading to him, and also sharing with others the task of writing down the blank verse which issued in increasing volume from his poetic muse.

In 1656 Milton married for the second time. But Katherine died only two years later, after giving birth to a daughter who survived only a few months. In 1663 he married for a third time – Elizabeth Minshull. To escape the plague in London they fled to Chalfont St. Giles. Though their stay there was brief – only about a year – it saw the completion of *Paradise Lost*. It was Milton's friend, Thomas Ellwood, who arranged for the Miltons to settle in the cottage at Chalfont St. Giles. And it is Ellwood who is reputed to have said to John Milton: 'Thou hast said much here of Paradise Lost, but what hast thou to say of paradise found?'. So Milton was moved to begin work at Chalfont on *Paradise Regained*. It was published soon after, alongside Samson Agonistes, when Milton returned to London in 1671. Three years later, Milton died.

William Cowper, to whom we turn next, once wrote of Milton:

'Greece, sound they Homer's, Rome thy Virgil's name,
But England's Milton equals both in fame.'

William Cowper (1731–1800)

Cowper is quintessentially a Bucks poet. He was not born in this county, but in the Rectory at Berkhamsted in the next-door county of Herts. And his last years were spent in Norfolk, where he died and is buried at East Dereham. But for nineteen years he lived at Olney, where his home, Orchardside House, is the Cowper Museum. And for nine years after that he lived in the nearby village of Weston Underwood. All his writing was done in those twenty-eight years of his life in Bucks.

Forever linked with Cowper is the name of John Newton, the former slave-trader who was converted from a life of profligacy and debauchery and who, after ordination, became Vicar of Olney. It was Newton who brought Cowper to Olney, and it was Newton who urged Cowper to find in poetry and in an evangelical faith a cure for his melancholia. Working together, the two produced the Olney Hymn Book – the first such Hymnal ever to be published in England (1779).

Many lives of Cowper have been written. All of them have to try to account for the alternating moods of tranquility and despair through which Cowper passed. As a child he was sensitive and hypochondriac. In early manhood he broke down completely and attempted suicide. He spent several months in Dr Cotton's Collegium Insanorum at St. Albans. Thereafter from time to time he suffered periods of acute melancholia which took a religious form. There was at least one other attempt at suicide.

The Cowper Museum, Olney. The poet lived here for 19 years. (JH)

Increasingly, greatly influenced by Newton, Cowper turned to evangelical Christianity for consolation. In an auto-biographical Memoir written in 1767 he wrote: 'Conviction of sin and expectation of instant judgement never left me'.

He was always profoundly affected by the deaths of those near and dear to him – his parents, especially his mother, his adopted father, the Reverend Morley Unwin, and Unwin's widow, Mary, and his brother. Storms and shipwrecks are images repeatedly reflected in his writing.

> *'Obscurest night involved the sky,*
> > *The Atlantic's billow roared,*
> *When such a destined wretch as I,*
> *Of friends, of hope, of all bereft,*
> > *His floating home forever left.'*

> *'No voice divine the storm allay'd,*
> > *No light propitious shone,*
> *When snatched from all effectual aid,*
> > *We perished each alone,*
> *But I beneath a rougher sea,*
> *And whelmed in deeper gulphs than he.'*

Yet the man who could pen such lines could also write with humour and with wit. His 'Diverting History of John Gilpin' achieved great popularity. And he caught the national mood when he wrote, in response to a great maritime disaster, 'The Loss of the Royal George'. No Poet Laureate could have done it better.

Nor was it only poetry he wrote. His gift for gentle satire found expression in 'Table Talk', and prompted Charles Lamb to write in a letter to Coleridge:

> 'I can forgive a man for not enjoying Milton, but I would not call that man my friend who should be offended by the "divine chit-chat" of Cowper.'

That tribute from Lamb to Cowper's genius is the more interesting when one remembers that Lamb, like Cowper, had known despair. His mood, too, could swing from melancholia to euphoria. Like Cowper, Charles Lamb also spent some time in an asylum. His sister, Mary, in a fit of madness, killed their mother. Yet brother and sister supported each other and together wrote for children their 'Tales from Shakespeare'. Both Lamb and Cowper show how thin is the dividing line between ecstasy and depression.

Cowper's poems, when he is not suffering from depression and melancholia, reflect calm tranquility and express his delicate feelings for nature. He has been called the precursor of Wordsworth as a poet of nature.

Thomas Gray (1716–1771)

Compared with his contemporary, Cowper, Gray's connection with Bucks was exceedingly brief. And it is only two poems that connect him forever with this County, his 'Ode on a Distant Prospect of Eton College' (1747), which forever unites Eton and the woodland lanes of Buckinghamshire; and his 'Elegy in a Country Churchyard' (1751).

In the churchyard at Stoke Poges is the tomb of Thomas Gray's mother, Dorothy. It bears the inscription:

> 'Dorothy Gray, the careful tender mother of many children, of whom one alone had the misfortune to survive her.'

That survivor was, of course, Thomas Gray who composed the epitaph. He died in 1771 at Cambridge, but is buried in his mother's grave at Stoke Poges.

Thomas Gray was born in London. His father, Philip Gray, was of so violent and jealous a nature that his wife was obliged to separate from him. She and her sister settled in Stoke Poges. Her poet son, Thomas, wrote many of his best verses while staying with his mother and aunt – most famously of course his 'Elegy in a Country Churchyard'.

> *The curfew tolls the knell of parting day,*
> *The lowing herd winds slowly o'er the lea,*
> *The ploughman homeward plods his weary way*
> *And leaves the world to darkness and to me.'*

The pastoral scene thus conjured up, is totally different today. Suburbanisation has taken over. But Gray's Memorial stands there in a ten-acre field preserved by the National Trust. The ancient church is still there, and a Garden of Remembrance adjoins the churchyard.

There is a story told about the British General James Wolfe. In the twilight of September 12th, 1759, on the eve of his victory on the Heights of Abraham against the French in Quebec, General Wolfe sat in a rowboat in the St. Lawrence River. He repeated the whole of Gray's 'Elegy' and then said: 'I would have preferred being the author of that poem to the glory of beating the French tomorrow morning'.

Next day he led his troops by a secret path to the Heights of Abraham above the city of Quebec and successfully drove off the French. But in storming the stronghold he himself was mortally wounded in his hour of victory. Gray's poem, which Wolfe so much admired, includes the line: 'The paths of glory lead but to the grave'.

Edmund Waller (1606—1687)
Waller was born at the Manor House at Coleshill near Amersham but lived mostly at Old Beaconsfield. He entered Parliament early. In 1631 he married a London heiress who died three years later.

When the Civil War began Waller was involved in a plot to seize London for the King. The plot failed and Waller was arrested and imprisoned. Only an abject apology saved him from execution. He was fined £10,000 and banished from the kingdom.

He was a poet who had political adroitness to match his poetic skills. He made his peace with Cromwell in 1651 and was allowed to return to England. And he was equally successful in making his peace with Charles II at the Restoration!

His ability to trim his sails is evidenced by the fact that in 1655 he published 'A Panegyric to My Lord Protector', and in 1660 he published 'To The King upon His Majesty's Happy Return!

As a poet he was praised by his fellows, notably by Dryden. Bucks born and bred, he undoubtedly counts as a Bucks poet, yet none of his verse is at all evocative of the Bucks landscape in the way that Cowper's is.

Edmund Spenser (1552–1599)

This Elizabethan poet and contemporary of Shakespeare has one cast-iron connection with Bucks – he was Secretary to Lord Grey de Wilton, Lord of the Manor of Whaddon in Bletchley. That much is fact.

A further LITERARY connection linking Spenser with Bucks is interesting but improbable. The claim is that Spenser wrote 'The Faerie Queen' beneath an ancient oak in the garden of Whaddon Hall. The historian Maxwell Fraser was convinced that this was so, but nobody else gives the story much credence.

But his employment as Secretary to Lord Grey of Whaddon Hall, Bletchley is undoubted. Lord Grey was plucked from a useful if obscure life at Whaddon in 1582 to fill the difficult post of Lord Deputy of Ireland. He took his young Secretary, Edmund Spenser, to Ireland with him.

Ireland proved as intractable to Lord Grey and his Secretary as it has continued to be intractable to many others since. Certainly Lord Grey was thankful when he could leave Ireland

and resume his life at Whaddon, where he died in 1593.

Edmund Spenser, probably kin to the Spencers of Althorp, fared rather better. He stayed on in Ireland where he was appointed one of the 'undertakers' for the settlement of Munster. He acquired Kilcolman Castle in Co. Cork. There he completed his work on 'The Faerie Queen' – work which Maxwell Fraser would maintain he had begun under that oak tree at Whaddon. It would be nice to think so.

George Lipscombe (1773–1846)

Dr George Lipscombe was a native of Quainton. His father was also a doctor, a medical officer in the Royal Navy who died in 1794. The young Dr Lipscombe married Mary George of Grendon Underwood. For a while the couple lived at Grendon and then moved to Quainton, and finally to Whitchurch. There the doctor practised his profession and was very much the Village Doctor, interested in people and not just in patients.

He had a great interest in all matters historical, especially in the history of his own county. He began to write about it. As his interest deepened and his writing continued, it became apparent that the historian in George Lipscombe was taking over from George Lipscombe the doctor.

What was taking shape now was a detailed History of Buckinghamshire. It was destined to become a monumental work in four great volumes, with an immense amount of detail on every aspect of Bucks history, ecclesiastical as well as secular.

But there was one great snag. The cost of compiling the History proved far greater that his own resources could bear. He moved to London, hoping that there he could find the support and backing which Whitchurch could not provide. But all in vain.

Lipscombe died in Westminster in 1846 in abject poverty. he would have been buried in a pauper's grave but for the kindness of a Mr Gyll of Wraysbury.

George Lipscombe's wife had died before him and there were no children to their marriage. He left behind him no estate or property *except* the fruits of his historical research, a huge quantity of material. A year after his death the work was published, and the four great volumes of the History of Buckinghamshire deservedly became the sort of standard County History which many Counties would envy and few could surpass.

William Cole (1714–1782)

George Lipscombe put Bucks into his debt by writing his great History of the county. William Cole had ambitions to do the same for the County of Cambridgeshire. He was an antiquary, a friend of Horace Walpole, and a high Tory Anglican clergyman. Writing to Walpole, Cole wrote of his manuscripts and his collection of notes and data.

> 'They are my only Delight; they are my wife and children; they have been, in short, my whole Employ and Amusement for these 20 or 30 Years. And though I really and sincerely think the greatest part of them Stuff and Trash, and deserves no other Treatment than the Fire, yet the Collection which I have made towards an History of Cambridgeshire . . . will be of singular Use to anyone who will have more Patience and Perseverance than I am Master of to put the Material together.'

What really stopped Cole from completing his History of Cambridgeshire was that Browne Willis, Lord of the Manors of Whaddon, Bletchley and Fenny Stratford, offered him the living of St. Mary's Church in Bletchley. Browne Willis, himself an Antiquary and Historian, wanted to have a fellow Antiquary in Bletchley Rectory. The effect was to stunt Cole's progress as an antiquary, but it made him a Diarist.

The Blecheley Diary

of the

Rev. WIlliam Cole

M.A. F.S.A.

Edited from the original MSS in the

British Museum.

Cole was Rector of Bletchley for fourteen years. His whole Diary, comprising more than a hundred manuscript volumes, was bequeathed by him to the British Museum on the condition 'that none of them may be inspected or looked into until twenty years after my decease'. One or two sections of the whole Diary have now been published, including The Blecheley (his spelling) Diary.

So we have this delightful account of how life was in the Parish of Bletchley, and in the surrounding countryside in North Bucks in the 1760s. Cole had a keen eye for character, and his Diary gives us profiles of many individuals – a gallery of portraits, including notables, both lay and clerical, as well as humbler folk.

He could be sardonic and scathing on occasions, and sometimes he confided to the Diary his scornful opinions of others, including sometimes the Bishop himself. His fellow clergy were not always spared, and he is highly critical of anything or anybody approaching dissent or nonconformity.

But the Diary, above all reveals a faithful parish priest, full of pastoral zeal for his people.

Benajmin Disraeli (1804–1881)
Disraeli takes his place elsewhere in these pages among the Men of State and Politics. Here we include him as a Man of Letters. As a writer he was prolific.

A short story by him was published when he was fifteen. His first novel was 'Vivian Grey', followed by no less than fifteen others. Besides the novels, there were also essays, and one biography (of Lord George Bentinck).

His earliest novels, like those of Walter Scott, were written to pay off debts. But by his last completed novel, 'Endymion', he could command enormous payments from publishers. When he died in 1881 he had finished only nine brief chapters of yet one more novel, to be called 'Falconet'.

The literary output from his home at Hughenden was prodigious. 'My works are my life', he once wrote. On another occasion he commented: 'When I want to read a novel, I write one'.

The Shelleys

Shelley and his wife, Mary, lived in many areas – in York, the Lake District, Dublin, and Italy. And for just one year, 1817, they made Marlow their home. While there, Percy Bysshe Shelley (1792–1822) wrote 'The Revolt of Islam', and also a political pamphlet, 'An Address to the People on the Death of Princess Charlotte'.

It was at Marlow also that Shelly's wife, Mary Wollstonecraft, (1797–1851) wrote her first novel, 'Frankenstein, or the Modern Prometheus'. In its Preface she explained how she and her husband, together with Byron, had spent the previous wet summer in Switzerland reading German ghost stories. All three agreed to write tales of the supernatural. But Mary Shelley was the only one to do so. She says that the concept for 'Frankenstein' came to her in a half-waking nightmare.

So from the tranquil reaches of the Thames where sunbeams chase the shadows over the meadows, and from the shades of Quarry woods we have 'The Revolt of Islam' from Shelley, and the Gothic tale of terror from his wife.

John Wilkes (1727–1797)

Prebendal House near the churchyard of Aylesbury's Parish Church was once the property of John Wilkes. It came to him through his marriage to Mary Mead, daughter of a wealthy London tradesman. By that marriage also in 1747 young John Wilkes (he was only twenty) also became the owner of Eaton Leys Farm and Mill at Water Eaton.

John Wilkes was born in 1727, the son of a wealthy distiller. As a rich young man John became a member of the notorious Hell Fire Club which celebrated its orgies at Medmenham Abbey, the home of Sir Francis Dashwood.

In 1757 Wilkes was elected MP for Aylesbury. It cost him £7,000 to buy the seat and a few years later he had to mortgage the Eaton Leys Farm. In 1761 he began a violent quarrel with Lord Bute, the Chief Minister of the young King George III. To develop his campaign against Bute he launched a weekly newspaper called The North Briton.

John Wilkes, drawn by Hogarth.

It was Issue 45 of The North Briton which caused the sensation. In it Wilkes wrote that the Speech from the Throne contained lies put into the King's mouth by his ministers. The Government was furious and issued warrants for the arrest not only of John Wilkes but also of the printers and publishers of The North Briton. So forty-eight were arrested. In Court Wilkes declined to answer on grounds of Parliamentary privilege, and the Judge agreed with him. Even more furious now, the Government were determined to get Wilkes on some other charge. He had earlier written and published privately a piece called 'Essay on Woman'. It was read aloud in the House of Lords and Their Lordships professed great moral indignation at its alleged obscenity. Wilkes was challenged to a duel in which he was wounded. All in all, Wilkes felt it would be politic to disappear for a while, so he fled to France. In his absence abroad he was expelled from the House of Commons and declared an Outlaw.

In 1768 he ventured back into Britain and stood for election in Middlesex. He won the seat but was not allowed to take it up. He was arrested and put in prison. Crowds demonstrated on his behalf outside the prison in St. George's Fields and riots broke out. The Scotch Regiment was sent in to quell the riot and six people were killed.

More riots followed and for a while it looked as if there would be a general insurrection. Wilkes, now out of prison, wrote an inflammatory piece about the massacre and was again arrested. His election as MP for Middlesex was quashed. Three more elections were attempted and each time Wilkes was elected but denied the seat.

By this time the whole of London was in an uproar. Apprentices and tradesmen marched and demonstrated on Wilke's behalf. Weavers, hatters, hat-dyers, tailors, watermen and glass-grinders all came out on strike. Merchant seamen joined in and brought the Port of London to a standstill. Coal-heavers marched on the Houses of Parliament.

Wilkes was finally released from prison in 1770. He continued his campaign for parliamentary freedom. Gradually he began to achieve success. In 1771 he was elected Sheriff of Middlesex, and in 1774 he became Lord Mayor of London. In that same year, too, he took his seat in Parliament at last without opposition.

When he died, on his tomb was inscribed the epitaph he had composed for himself. Just six words:

JOHN WILKES A FRIEND OF LIBERTY.

Edmund Burke (1729–97)

Burke was an exact contemporary of Wilkes. This Irish statesman, philosopher and political thinker had no ancestral connection with Bucks. But he acquired the estate of Gregories, near Beaconsfield, and became MP for Wendover in 1768.

For more than a quarter of a century – 1768–1797 – the quiet of the Bucks countryside, and its rural occupations into which he entered with great zest, gave him enormous satisfaction.

But the purchase of Gregories also brought him endless financial anxieties. Even so, Gregories was the memorable resort of statesmen, politicians and men of letters. An additional interest and preoccupation for Burke was his concern for the education of the children of French emigres. He established a house on the road to Wycombe where they could be educated and he often rode over there from Beaconsfield to visit them.

He became Private Secretary to the Prime Minister, the Marquis of Rockingham, and soon began to put pen to paper to express his philosophical/political views. Great issues of the day engaged his attention and prompted his writings, including the breakaway of the American Colonies, the French Revolution, and the Wilkes controversy.

He died in 1797 and is buried in the little church at Beaconsfield. He ranks as one of the foremost political thinkers of England. He had a vast knowledge of affairs, a lively imagination, and a passionate range of sympathies. Yet, as a speaker, as opposed to a writer, he was awkward and ungainly. The House of Commons tended to empty when he rose to speak! But his writings speak for him.

One often-quoted saying of his was:

'Men will never look forward to posterity who never look back to their ancestors.'

Yet others who are part of Bucks literary heritage are:

> RICHARD SHERIDAN (1751–116).
> The dramatist lived for a while at East Burnham.
> ALISON UTTLEY (1884–1976),
> author of more than eighty-seven books for children, lived at Beaconsfield.
> ENID BLYTON (1900–1968),
> the world's best-selling children's author, lived at Bourne End and Beaconsfield.
> G. K. CHESTERTON (1874–1936).
> He wrote much of his best work, including the 'Father Brown' stories while living at Beaconsfield.
> ROALD DAHL (1916–1990),
> lived for a while at Great Missenden.
> T. S. ELIOT (1888–1965),
> lived for a short while at Marlow.
> EDGAR WALLACE (1875–1932).
> He wrote more than 150 novels and 15 plays. He is buried in Little Marlow Cemetery.

Chapter 5

Men of the Cloth

Originally the 'cloth' used to be applied to the customary garb of any calling, meaning 'livery'. But by the 17th century the 'cloth' became restricted to the clergy and the clerical office.

Here are some of the Men of the Cloth who down the centuries have figured in Bucks history. Perhaps listing them in strict chronological order we shall be saved from the necessity of apportioning to them degrees of praise or blame!

1275

SIMON de REDA became Prior of Tickford Priory near Newport Pagnell. He was a thoroughly disreputable person, ruling a Priory whose laxity more than once earned the stern reprimands of the Bishop of Lincoln. De Reda was finally deposed in 1291 on the serious charges of 'waste of goods, evil living, and homcide'!

1290

JOHN SCHORNE came from Monks Risborough to North Marston as Rector. He served the parish until his death in 1314. He earned a great reputation not only for his piety, but also for his skill in water divining, and for healing the sick. His fame spread far and wide. His tomb in North Marston Church became a Shrine to which pilgrims flocked in great numbers. It was said that only Walsingham and Canterbury attracted more pilgrims.

Part of the legend built up around John Schorne was that he possessed the power to control the Devil by 'conjuring him into a boot'. Several inns adopted the 'Devil in the Boot' motif for their inn-signs.

The pilgrim traffic to North Marston brought the village and its church a considerable income. Schorne was never canonised as a saint, though many revered him as such.

All that remains of John Schorne's Shrine in North Marston Church. (NK)

Towards the end of the 15th century the King wanted a new St. George's Chapel to be built at Windsor. He had already appointed the Bishop of Salisbury as Dean of Windsor and he commissioned the Dean to create the new Chapel. The Dean decided that to raise the money needed for the project, he must find a way of attracting pilgrims to Windsor. For that to happen, he needed a magnet – a holy shrine – to draw the pilgrims there. He thought that moving John Schorne's Shrine from North Marston to Windsor would serve the purpose very well. So he successfully applied to the Pope for permission to move John Schorne's bones to Windsor. Windsor's gain was North Marston's loss.

1349

On Maundy Thursday night in 1349 the Vicar of Stantonbury, WALTER de BASCHESHES walked in the darkness towards his church. As he stretched out his hand to open the door he drew back in alarm. For there, on the door's central panel he saw a gargoyle so hideous that for a moment he was transfixed in horror. In desperation he hurried into the church and threw holy water from the holy water stoup on the apparition. Then he passed out!

He was found next day, Good Friday, lying insensible on the floor of the church. When he recovered, he tried to explain what had happened. Asking for charcoal, he sketched a likeness of the terrible apparition he had seen.

The story of this strange occurrence spread far and wide and became the basis for the Stanton Legend. The Cult of the Holy Door of Stantonbury even drew King Henry V – he rode over from Windsor to see for himself the place where it had happened. Even as late as 1591 Queen Elizabeth's Court of High Commission gave orders that the old door should be pannelled on the side where the apparition was alleged to have appeared, and that in future the door should remain open.

1368

JOHN WYCLIFF, 'the Morning Star of the Reformation', was

presented to the living of Ludgershall. He exchanged his previous and richer living of Fillingham in Lincolnshire so that he might be nearer Oxford. Wycliff held the living of Ludgershall for eight years, until in 1376 he went to be Rector of Lutterworth.

During his tenancy at Ludgershall, although he spent most of his time in Oxford, he preached in the market towns of Bucks. Many of his followers (the Lollards) suffered martyrdom at Amersham and elsewhere. Wycliff

Wycliff. His followers were known as Lollards.

was a powerful opponent of the claims of the Papacy. He also wrote a series of works attacking the wealth of the Church. He emphasised various points which were later central to the Reformation. He argued that only Scripture offered a firm base for authority, and therefore the Scriptures must be available to all in their own language.

In 1381, by which time he was at Lutterworth, his opinions were declared heretical in Oxford and his trial was demanded. Before he could be tried he died at Lutterworth in 1384 and was buried there. But later his remains were dug up, burnt, and flung in to the River Swift at Lutterworth.

1378

On June 4th one Lawrence Thetcher found the body of WILLELMUM SAPCOTE dead on the highway. Sapcote had been the Parson of Little Loughton since 1369. An inquest was held and the jury found that Sapcote had been feloniously killed by an arrow shot at him by JOHN GERVYES, the Priest of Great Loughton. Gervyes fled to his own church to claim sanctuary there.

1509

In this year WILLIAM OF WARHAM married Henry VIII to Catherine of Aragon. William was a Lawyer by training and had been Master of the Rolls. As a Priest, he was rector of Great Horwood though he never lived there. The parish was looked after by a curate whom William appointed and paid.

William went on to become Chancellor of England and Archbishop of Canterbury. It was in that latter capacity that he had married Henry VIII and Catherine. When, later Henry wanted to divorce Catherine, Archbishop Warham tried to oppose him.

1540

The Cistercian Woburn Abbey had been founded in 1145. In 1540, in common with all other Religious Houses, it was dissolved. The last Abbot of Woburn was ROBERT HOBS. When his Abbey was closed he was not just turned out into the world – he was hanged, from an oak tree outside the main gate of the Abbey. This was because Hobs had publicly questioned the King's supremacy in Church matters.

THOMAS ANDREWS was the Parish Priest of Addington in the 16th century. When Henry VIII renounced the supremacy of the Pope over the English Church he ordered that all the old Catholic Prayer books should be destroyed. Andrews in conscience couldn't do it. So he hid his six Catholic prayer books by walling them up in the north wall of the Chancel. He also hid a small 14th century 'super Altar'. The six books and the 'mensa' remained hidden for nearly three hundred years and they only came to light by accident in 1857 when part of the Church was being rebuilt. The slate slab was let into the Altar of Addington Church when the restoration as carried out. (A later Vicar of Addington was the Rev. Gerard Olivier. He became Vicar in 1924, just at the time when his teenage son, Lawrence Olivier, was about ready to go to Drama School in London. For several years he had been choirboy and acolyte in his father's churches. So these had been the first public performances of the future great theatrical knight, or rather, Peer, Lord Olivier.)

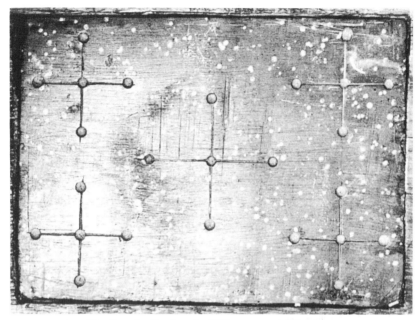

The Super-altar lost for 300 years at Addington.

1609–70

What sort of Man of the Cloth was RICHARD CARPENTER? He was certainly originally a Roman Catholic, born in Newport Pagnell. On a visit to Rome, it is said, he was commissioned by the Pope to return to England and under the auspices of the Benedictines to work for England's conversion.

Oddly, however, on his return to England, he became an Anglican! But later he changed again, and became an Independent Minister. He now vigorously attacked both Anglicans and Baptists. His preaching met with most success in and around Aylesbury. He died in 1670 and at the end of his life he had returned once more to the Roman fold.

1616

WILLIAM BREDON became Rector of Thornton and served the parish for twenty-two years, dying in 1638. He assisted Sir Christopher Heydon in writing his book, 'Judicial Astrology'.

Astrology was a major pre-occupation with William Bredon. He claimed to be able to predict any person's future by studying the zodiacal data obtaining at the time of birth, and by studying the configuration of planets at a particular moment. In other words, Bredon was offering the same service 350 years ago as is nowadays offered by the astrologers who write the columns on 'What the Stars Foretell' in the newspapers.

1646

ANTHONY TYRINGHAM, Rector of Tyringham Parish, was a member of the Tyringham family which held the Manor of that name, and with it the advowson, or right to appoint clergy to the parish.

Over the centuries three of the Rectors of Tyringham parish were themselves members of the Tyringham family. Of these, Anthony was the one who was caught up in the trauma and drama of the Civil War.

In 1646 he and two companions had the misfortune to be seized by rebel soldiers on the road near Stony Stratford. Despite his clerical attire, Anthony was brutally assaulted by the Roundheads who slashed his head with a sword and also cut across his fingers. Later, as the prisoners were being hustled away towards Aylesbury, Anthony was again assaulted with a sword which almost severed his arm. At Whitchurch he was stripped of his boots and jerkin and by the time Aylesbury was reached he was in a sorry state. Next day his arm had to be amputated (without benefit of anaesthesia which had not yet been invented). Anthony survived nevertheless. He died in 1659 at Tyringham where he is buried.

1660

JOSEPH NEWELL was 'Rector' of the Parish of Thornborough for nearly thirty years, from 1660 to 1688. The 'Rector' is written thus in inverted commas because in fact Joseph Newell was bogus. He wasn't a parson and he never had been! Yet for all those twenty-eight years he ran the parish, administering the Sacraments of Baptism and Holy Communion, and doing all the things that a parson does.

His deceit only came to light in 1688 when he was 'detected for Want of Orders'. He was ordered to retire and to leave the parish. He moved to live at Pottersbury and there he died.

1660–68

Between these years BENJAMIN KEACH was Pastor of the tiny Baptist Chapel in Winslow. He had been born and baptised in an Anglican family at Stoke Hammond but experienced conversion in his teens under the influence of JOHN RUSSELL, the Baptist Minister at Chesham.

Keach's Meeting House, Winslow. (JH)

At the age of twenty Keach began his ministry at Winslow. In the Chapel there a tablet commemorates him thus:

'BENJAMIN KEACH Born 1640 Died 1704.
Pastor of the Baptist Church assembling in this place
from 1660 to 1668, who restored congregational
singing of hymns as a part of Divine Worship and
suffered in Prison and in the Pillory here and at
Aylesbury in October 1664 for asserting the right of
Liberty and Conscience and bearing witness to THE
SOVEREIGNTY OF CHRIST'

In 1668 with his family Keach moved to London. They were set on by highwayman *en route* and robbed of everything they possessed. Keach spent the next thirty years of his life in the Baptist Ministry in London. He died in 1704 and is buried in Southwark.

Keach in the stocks, still preaching!

1674

In this year JOHN MASON came to Water Stratford as Vicar. He stayed there till his death in 1694. His Hell-Fire preaching brought crowds flocking to the village. He was convinced that the Second Coming was imminent and that when it occurred only the village of Water Stratford would be spared. This caused many from elsewhere to sell up their homes and to move to Water Stratford.

For weeks on end a sort of corporate madness seized the village. Mason had announced that though he would die, he would rise again after three days. After his burial people claimed that they had seen him. His successor felt obliged to open up his grave to demonstrate that the dead Vicar was still in it. It took several years before Water Stratford returned to any sort of normality.

1693

LEWIS ATTERBURY was Rector of the tiny village and parish of Milton Keynes (which nearly three hundred years later would give its name to the great new city of Milton Keynes).

In 1693 Lewis Atterbury was riding his horse, returning from London to his village. Passing over the bridge at Newport Pagnell he was swept into the river and drowned during a great flood. (For what happened to his son, also a priest, see page 112.)

1714–82

WILLIAM COLE spent fourteen of his sixty-eight years as Rector of St. Mary's Church in Bletchley. He was a great Diarist and his 'Blecheley (his spelling) Diary' gives a wonderful insight into life in North Bucks in the 18th century. (See page 54.)

The name of another parson has its place in Cole's story. He was RALPH LEYCESTER, the Parish Priest of Fenny Stratford. Cole had appointed him to that office and he came to regret it. Leycester was an obstinate and cantankerous character. Cole complained about him several times to the Bishop of Lincoln but the Bishop either couldn't or wouldn't take action. It was Leycester who had the last word. He had been appointed to Fenny Stratford in 1760. Cole finally left Bletchley in 1767, but his *bete noir* Leycester, stayed on in Fenny Stratford till 1793.

1764

For further reference to JOHN NEWTON see page 48. His uniqueness is that from being a debauched and blasphemous slave trader he was converted to become a priest. For sixteen years he was Vicar of Olney, the friend of Cowper the poet. Together they wrote and published the Olney Hymn Book.

Newton transferred to London and served for twenty-eight more years in the Parish of St. Mary Woolnoth. There he was of considerable help to William Wilberforce in the MP's long struggle to get slavery and the slave trade abolished. Though Newton was at first buried in London his remains were later transferred to a tomb at Olney.

1766

The Reverend Mr RISELY, Rector of Tingewick, was put on trial for manslaughter. He happened one day to witness a highwayman holding up a traveller just outside Stony Stratford. He went at once to the victim's assistance. The two together then chased the highwayman, calling on him repeatedly to stop.

The Rector, either by a remarkably good shot, or by chance, hit the fleeing highwayman, shooting him dead. That was the charge that brought him into court. The Duke of Grafton, hearing the case, had no hesitation in acquitting him. More than that, he was so impressed by the Rector's prowess that he offered him a better living at Ashton in Northamptonshire.

1777

Not many parsons have been hanged at Tyburn. One who was is the Reverend Dr WILLIAM DODD. He was hanged at Tyburn on June 17th 1777 at the age of forty-eight.

Dodd lived in London, way beyond his means. He had his own Chapel in London and was one of the most celebrated preachers of his day. His connection with Bucks is two-fold: he was the absentee Rector both of Wing and of Chalgrove. (He also held the living of Hockliffe.)

WILLIAM DODD, LL. D.

The Rev. William Dodd, hanged at Tyburn

These country livings were of importance to Dodd because of the tithes they brought him. In his absence poorly-paid curates actually looked after the parishes.

Dodd was living so far beyond his means that he succumbed to the temptation to forge a Bond in the name of the Earl of Chesterfield, to whose godson he was tutor. The forgery was easily detected. The offence, being one of the very many in those days for which capital punishment was enjoined, cost the life of Sr William Dodd, on that June day in 1777.

1814–57

The Rector at Passenham was LORAINE SMITH. He was elegant, he was amiable, and he was a sportsman – with particular enthusiasm for prize fighting.

This latter enthusiasm might have caused embarrassment to Loraine Smith because, not only was he a parson, he was also a Magistrate, and Prize Fighting was illegal. But he seems to have found ways to combine all three elements.

1876

This year takes us back to an individual already noted at North Marston in 1290, the blessed John Schorne.

In the 1870s Dr S. R. JAMES came as Vicar to North Marston. In 1874 he established Schorne College in the village. It had about ninety boys, aged 9–15. They were taught by various members of the Vicar's family.

They published a joint School and Parish magazine called the Schornonian. Schorne College lasted from 1874 to 1912. Ironically, given the healing miracles attributed to Blessed John Schorne almost exactly six hundred years before, it was an outbreak of cholera in 1912 which caused Schorne College to close.

1909–46

To end this survey of Men of the Cloth who in their various ways over the centuries have been figures in our Bucks landscape, we come now to a 20th century parson. He was NEWMAN GUEST, an eccentric Irishman who was Vicar of St. James Church, New Bradwell, for thirty-seven years (1906–1946). So his ministry included the years of both World Wars. Many can still remember him and recall how, wearing his old plimsolls and riding his old bike, he would coast down the hills with his feet up on either side of the front mudguard.

He astonished his congregation at Evensong one Sunday in 1909 by telling them that many of them were living in sin and that their children were illegitimate! Having sprung this bombshell, he went on to explain. St. James Church was built in 1860 to take over from the ancient parish church at Stanton Low. This was to help with the great housing development occasioned by the creation of Wolverton Railways Works.

Unfortunately, while it was well understood that the pastoral responsibilities had passed from the ancient parish church at Stanton Low to the new church in New Bradwell, nobody had technically conveyed from the old church to the new the right to administer the Sacrament of Holy Matrimony!

So from 1860 to 1909 any marriages which had taken place in the new church were, technically, invalid. A frantic search of the Registers revealed that there had been 424 such marriages. Furthermore, any offspring from those marriages, were, technically, illegitimate! And there had been well over two hundred such births!

Fr. Guest, having no doubt enjoyed springing his bombshell, of course went on to explain that a Provisional Order in Council was being passed by the Government. This would certify, retroactively, that all those previous marriages could be regarded as valid, and all the offspring resulting from them could be regarded as legitimated.

Chapter 6

Men of Wealth

The Rothschilds Squirearchy

The name Rothschild literally means 'Red Shield', and a red shield was the signboard of the house of a moneylender in Frankfort. To that moneylender was born a son in 1743 named Meyer Amschel Rothschild. He rose to be a financier of growing international repute and ability. He became financial adviser to the Landgrave of Hesse.

The House of Rothschild soon became important in the service of foreign governments. It handled the transmission of money from the British Government to Wellington in Spain. And it negotiated loans for the Danish Government.

All five sons of Meyer Amschel Rothschild were made Barons of the Austrian Empire in 1822. The eldest son, Anselm Meyer, succeeded as Head of the House in Frankfort. Of the other four sons, Solomon established a branch of the firm in Vienna; Nathan Meyer did the same in London; Charles opened a branch in Naples, and James in Paris.

In the 19th century the House of Rothschild was involved in many great government loans. It became first of the banking houses of the world. Nathan Meyer in London took the lead in these developments. He staked his fortune on the success of Britain in the war against Napoleon. The moment he received news of Wellington's victory at Waterloo he bought and sold stock which brought him a profit of over a million pounds.

While the Rothschild family continued to be thoroughly international, the English branch of the family, founded by Nathan Meyer, soon put down roots in this country. Anthony

Rothschild received a baronetcy in 1846 and became Baron Rothschild in 1885.

The Rothschild headquarters were of course in London, but the family chose Buckinghamshire as the county in which they wished to establish their homes. Their interest in Bucks was prompted by the nearness of the county to London, but also by their enthusiasm for country sport in general, and in hunting, stag hunting in particular. They began by renting property in Bucks, and then one by one purchasing land and building their own country mansions.

Statutum de Judaismo

This was the shameful Statute which was passed in 1270. Quite simply, it prohibited Jews from owning land. It was not repealed until 1846, though for some time before that it was largely ignored.

When the Rothschilds were established in England it was Sir Anthony Rothschild who decided in 1851 to make his home in Buckinghamshire. He acquired a magnificent mansion at ASTON CLINTON. Later, other members of the family, including Baron Ferdinand, followed his example.

By the end of the century no less than five Rothschild mansions had been established in Bucks. As well as Aston Clinton, these were MENTMORE TOWERS, ASCOTT HOUSE, HALTON HOUSE, and WADDESDON. Of these, without doubt, Waddesdon Manor was the flagship.

Mentmore Towers

This great house was the first of the five mansions built in Buckinghamshire by members of the Rothschild family in the 19th century. Baron Mayer de Rothschild began making extensive purchases of land round the village Mentmore in 1830. In 1850 he bought the manor itself and decided to create at Mentmore a purpose-built mansion on a lavish scale. It was to be not only a great residence, but also a worthy setting for the great art treasures that would be assembled there.

The building began in 1852 and took three years to

complete. The chosen architect was George Stokes. There was a conscious decision to base the design of the house on Woolaton Hall near Nottingham, but the end result was a building that greatly outdid its model. Though George Stokes was the architect, his father-in-law actually supervised the work. He was Joseph Paxton who had just won great fame as the architect of the Crystal Palace, designed and built for the Great Exhibition in 1851 in Hyde Park.

The great house built at Mentmore introduced features hitherto unknown in domestic architecture, including provision for constant hot water and for artificial ventilation. While the great house was being built the Baron turned his attention to its setting. A seven hundred acre park was laid out, and the village of Mentmore was virtually rebuilt. The ancient parish church was also put in order.

The Baron also built extensive stables, and kennels for his staghounds. His Stud was at Crafton. At Ledburn a hostel was built to house trainers and stable lads. Horse racing and staghounds were of passionate interest to the Baron. On the

Mentmore Towers. (NK)

Turf he had many successes including winning the Derby and the St. Ledger.

Equally passionate was his love of art. The new great mansion was filled with treasures from all over Europe, particularly from Amsterdam and from Paris.

But Mayer de Rothschild did not have long to enjoy all that he had achieved at Mentmore. He died in 1874 and he had no son to succeed him. His widow, Lady Rothschild died only three years after her husband, in 1877.

This left their daughter, Hannah, as sole heir. She proved an energetic inheritor, with a very special interest in education. At Wingrave she built a fine village school, together with thirty new houses for the villagers, many of whom worked on the Mentmore estate.

Wingrave remains a most attractive village. It has a fine 13th century church and there are a number of 15th and 16th century houses and farm buildings. There is also a large rambling Victorian mansion which has had an interesting history. It used to be called Wingrave Manor and in World War II it was the home of the exiled Czech Government. After the war its name was changed to Mount Tabor and it became the home of Anglican nuns who ran a home there for women and girls. Later, once more known as Wingrave Manor it became a home for the disabled.

Enter Rosebery

But back to the story of Mentmore Towers itself. In 1878 Hannah married Archibald Primrose, fifth Earl of Rosebery. he was then a young man of thirty-one, and was destined to become a future Prime Minister (1894). Their London wedding was the social event of the year in 1878. Disraeli gave the bride away, and the distinguished guest list was headed by the Prince of Wales.

The Roseberys had always been a great sporting family. So when the newly-weds came to live at Mentmore the tradition of success on the Turf, begun by Baron Meyer de Rothschild, was still further enhanced. The Baron had won the Derby twice; his son-in-law, Lord Rosebery, went on to win it three more times. In the grounds at Mentmore an equine cemetery was started where many famous horses which had carried the Rosebery colours lie buried.

The Roseberys have other residences, at Dalmeny in Scotland and at Newmarket. In 1978 they decided to move from Mentmore. A series of sales of the fabulous art treasures attracted enormous attention. The great house itself was bought by the Transcendental Meditation Movement to serve as its Headquarters.

There is still limited access for the public to visit Mentmore Towers – between 1.45pm and 4pm on Sundays and Bank Holiday Mondays.

Manorial History
Mentmore Towers is 'only' 140 years old. But its pre-Rothschild history stretches back nearly one thousand years before the Baron appeared. Before the Conquest the Manor of Mentmore with Ledburne belonged to Edith, the wife of King Edward the Confessor. At the Conquest it passed to Hugh Lupus, the Earl of Chester. From his family it passed to the Zouche family of Harringworth.

Several generations of the Zouche family held the manor right up to the 15th century. The sitting Zouche owner at that time was John Lord Zouche. In the bitter struggle between the Yorkists and the Lancastrians (the Wars of the Roses), John Lord Zouche was a supporter of Richard III. Richard, at the Battle of Bosworth in 1485, lost the battle, his life and his throne. The victor was Henry VII. The Mentmore lands having been escheated to the crown after Bosworth, were bestowed by the new king on Sir Reginald Bray.

The Bray family was one of great antiquity. Reginald Bray played a principal part in the negotiations between the rival houses of York and Lancaster. For this he was suitably rewarded. Mentmore with Ledburne Manor became his along with many other manors. He was made a Banneret, was taken into the new King's Council, and raised to the Honour of the Garter.

Having no son of his own to succeed him, Sir Reginald Bray adopted Edmund, eldest son of his younger brother John, as his heir. In later years the succession did not go smoothly and there were many disputes.

By the middle of the 16th century the Brays, like many others, were torn between supporting Queen Mary I, or her half-sister Elizabeth. Lord Bray was accused of having been heard to say: 'If my neighbour of Hatfield (the Princess, afterwards Queen, Elizabeth) might once reign, I should have my lands and debts given me once again, which I both wish and trust once to see'. Such words could have cost him his life. However, he was pardoned and was entrusted by Queen Mary with the command of English troops in yet another battle against the French in the seemingly never-ending French Wars. That was in 1557. He won the battle in France but in that campaign he contracted an illness and died soon after his return.

No Great House Before the Towers?

Though one speaks of Manors such as Mentmore throughout these long centuries, it was land rather than great houses which the manors represented. There would, of course, have been houses built in the 15th and 16th centuries, but there was no single 'great house' at Mentmore. The various owners of the land, having other manors elsewhere besides Mentmore, leave no record of having owned or lived in a 'great house' at Mentmore itself. It was the ownership of the land that mattered – that and the advowson which went with the ownership. (Advowson was the right of the Lord of the Manor to appoint clergy to the livings of the parishes in their estates.)

Such was the situation in the 19th century when, as we have seen, Baron Meyer de Rothschild began in 1830 to buy up land on a huge scale in North Bucks. When he finally bought the Manor of Mentmore itself in 1850 he was able to put in hand his great scheme to create Mentmore Towers.

Waddesdon Manor

This National Trust stately home near Aylesbury is very special for a number of reasons. It is a magnificent French Renaissance-style chateau; it is a positive treasure house of great works of art (Reynolds, Gainsborough, Romney, Fragonard, Greuze, Boucher and others); it houses one of the finest collection of Sevres porcelain anywhere; there is much very fine furniture; and the Park, with its formal gardens and rococo-style aviary completes the picture.

Waddesdon Manor was built between 1874 and 1879 by Baron Ferdinand de Rothschild. Baron Ferdinand did more than build a home in Buckinghamshire. He identified himself with every aspect of life in his adopted country. He became a

Waddesdon Manor.

Justice of the Peace, a Member of the County Council, High Sheriff, and MP for Aylesbury. In fact the Aylesbury constituency was represented by members of the Rothschild family from 1865 to 1923. One of them, Nathaniel, went to the House of Lords as the first Lord Rothschild.

What Baron Ferdinand de Rothschild achieved at Waddesdon reflected his great knowledge and love of French 18th century art. He wanted to create a house and a setting worthy of the collection he intended to assemble. To achieve this he employed the French architect Gabriel Hippolyte Distailleur who designed for him the great chateau-like mansion we see today. Similarly, for the Park, he employed the French landscape gardener, Laine. The results speak for themselves.

Ferdinand died in 1898, leaving Waddesdon to his sister, Miss Alice de Rothschild. Like her brother, Miss Alice was a knowledgeable and enthusiastic art collector, especially of Sevres and Meisen china. So in her time Waddesdon was still further enriched.

She died in 1922, leaving Waddesdon to her great-nephew, James de Rothschild. This made a link with the French branch of the family, for James was the son of Baron Edmund de Rothschild of Paris. This still further enriched the fabulous art treasures of Waddesdon, because James inherited from his father valuable art treasures comprising paintings, furniture, and yet more china.

James died in 1957. In his will he bequeathed Waddesdon with all its magnificent art treasures to the National Trust, together with an endowment to make sure that both the house and its fabulous contents could be maintained.

That, then, is the story of Waddesdon Manor. But of course there is a very long pre-Rothschild history to consider also. For Waddesdon dates back a thousand years to the time of the Norman Conquest and to Domesday.

It is strange, though, that there is no history of any earlier buildings at Waddesdon – no medieval or Elizabethan Manor House. The great Rothschild Mansion was the first.

In pre-Norman times Waddesdon and its surrounding hamlets belonged to Queen Edith and was in the hands of her tenant, Brictric. By the time of the Domesday Survey it was listed as held by Milo Crispin.

But the really significant name to emerge in that far-off period was Courtenay. The name first appears in the Charter-List of Battle Abbey as being among those who were prominent at William's side when he successfully invaded England in 1066.

In the distribution of lands with which the Conqueror rewarded his supporters, Courtenay was awarded the Manor of Waddesdon along with countless other manors, most of them in the west country. Members of the Courtenay family were created Earls of Devon. Reginald de Courtenay held Waddesdon in the 12th century. He died in 1194, but Waddesdon continued in his family for ten more generations.

It was held by Thomas, 5th Earl of Devon who died in 1548. His was a tragic family. Of his three sons, Thomas the eldest (6th Earl of Devon) was taken prisoner at the Battle of Towton Field in 1460 and beheaded; Henry, the second son, was beheaded at Salisbury; John the youngest son was killed at Tewkesbury. The grandson, Thomas, was attainted and his estates were forfeited to the Crown. The Waddesdon estate was recovered by another branch of the family through Edward Courtenay who was restored to the Earldom of Devon. But tragedy continued. Edward's son was attainted in 1539, and once again Waddesdon among other places, was escheated to the Crown.

In 1540 Henry VIII leased parts of the Waddesdon land to Edward Lambourne, and in the same year the King granted the Manor of Waddesdon with all its rights to John Goodwyn.

The Goodwyns were an ancient Buckinghamshire family. Their Mansion was at Wooburn. Jane, a daughter of Arthur Goodwyn, married Philip, 4th Lord Wharton. In 1637 Lord Wharton inherited all the Goodwyn estates both at Wooburn and at Winchendon, where he lived. He was succeeded by Thomas, 5th Lord Wharton.

After the Whartons the Manor of Waddesdon passed to the Duke of Marlborough, and it was from the Duke of Marlborough that Baron Ferdinand de Rothschild purchased Waddesdon together with more than two thousand acres.

This necessarily condensed recital of Waddesdon's history between the Conquest in the 11th century and the coming of the Rothschilds in the 19th century has revealed no mention of any house, great or otherwise, during that long period – until the building of the present great house.

This is the more surprising because a closer look at the lineage of the Courtenays, Earls of Devon, reveals the extent to which their origins were so closely bound up with the Conqueror's own family. They trace their ancestry back to Richard, Duke of Normandy, the great-grandfather of the Conqueror himself. And Alfreda, a niece of the Conqueror, also married into their family. Another connection by marriage wa to Robert Fitz-Edith, a natural son of Henry I.

Despite these royal connections, although Waddesdon Manor figured in the lists of holdings of succeeding landowners, none of them seem ever to have built at Waddesdon any residence of note – until Baron Ferdinand de Rothschild, that is. The magnificence of *his* building certainly makes up for the lack of any predecessor.

Ascott House

Ascott House at Wing near Leighton Buzzard is a National Trust property. It was bought by Leopold de Rothschild as a country house in 1874. But the origins of the estate date back to at least the 12th century. A Priory then existed at Wing as a cell of Benedictine monks attached to the Abbey of St. Nicholas of Angers.

At the end of the 14th century Sir Hugh Luttrell, a kinsman of King Henry IV, was awarded an annual income from lands belonging to the Priory at Wing. He held high offices of state and in 1402 was Lieutenant of Calais and he served in key positions in the French wars. Though awarded the annuity from the priory lands at Wing, he lived and died at Dunster Castle in Somerset.

In the 15th century Ascott Manor was passed to Thomas Rokes and thereafter to his heirs. But in 1528 King Henry VIII granted the Manor of Wing to Cardinal Wolsey. When all priories and monasteries were suppressed the revenues from Wing and Ascott also went to Cardinal Wilsey. The Cardinal planned to devote these revenues to his College, called Cardinal College, in Oxford. However, Wolsey fell from favour when he proved unwilling to support Henry's divorce from Catherine of Aragon. The King then granted to Sir Robert Dormer the Manors of Wing, Ascott, Burcot and Crofton.

So began the long Dormer regime at Wing which lasted from the 15th to the 18th century. Many monuments in Wing Church reflect the Dormer succession. On the north side of the chancel there is a monument to Sir William Former, who died in 1575, and his wife Dorothy. Below are their children, some of them shown as babes who died in infancy. On the other side is the monument to Sir Robert Dormer and Dame Elizabeth his wife. Both figures are kneeling.

There is also a monumental brass in the south aisle. It is dated 1648. It is to the memory of Thomas Cotes who was Porter at Ascott Hall. He is represented as kneeling with a Porter's staff under his feet. He wears a high-crowned hat and a large key is to be seen lying behind him. The inscription runs:

'Honest old Thomas Cotes, that sometime was Porter at Ascott
Hall, hath now (alas) Left his Key, Lodg, Fyre, Friends and
all to have a Roome in Heaven. This is that good man's grave.
Reader prepare for thine, For none can tell
But that you Two may meete tonight. Farewell.'
Set up at the apoyntment and charges of his friend
Geo. Houghton.

The Dormer name changes frequently during the three centuries of their tenancy, as titles and honours were gained and marriages took place. Thus one learns to identify various members of the Dormer lineage at various times as Baron Dormer, Viscount Ascott, Earl of Carnavon, and Earl of Chesterfield.

In the reign of Charles I the sitting Dormer was the Earl of Carnavon. He put in hand an extension to the old Manor House on a plan of Inigo Jones, but the plan was never entirely carried through. In the following century, from 1720 onwards, the house deteriorated and became somewhat ruinous. At the same time the surrounding park was greatly neglected and the timber cut down.

But long before that Ascott House had its moments of prominence in the nation's history. It is often a source of amusement to recount the improbable number of houses and beds in which Queen Elizabeth is said to have slept. Ascott House at Wing is genuinely one of them, though she was not yet Queen when she slept there. It happened in 1554 and Queen Mary, the daughter of Catherine of Aragon was on the throne. Her half-sister Elizabeth, daughter of Anne Boleyn, was virtually a prisoner at Woodstock. It was decided to bring her to London, and it was on that journey from Woodstock to the capital that she slept at Ascott House. Four years later Queen Mary died and the Princess Elizabeth who had slept that night in Ascott House became Queen Elizabeth I.

In the Civil War of 1642 to 1649 Ascott House suffered grievously. The Mansion was ransacked by the Parliamentarians, documents were seized, and the inmates of the house were very roughly handled. Robert Dormer, who had been created Viscount Ascott in 1628, was a stalwart supporter of Charles I. He fought with great bravery at the Battle of Newbury in 1653 in which he lost his life.

The title of Earl of Carnavon and Viscount Ascott became extinct when Charles, the second Earl of Carnavon, died leaving no male issue, despite his having married three times. His daughter married Philip, Earl of Chesterfield. So the Manor of Wing passed thereby to the Earl of Chesterfield.

If the history of Ascott House is the story of the Dormer lineage from the 15th to the 18th century, in the 19th and 20th centuries a quite different and international lineage took its place – the House of Rothschild. In 1847 Baron Meyer de Rothschild established kennels at Wing for his staghounds.

And in 1874 Leopold de Rothschild bought Ascott House as a family hunting lodge.

The house he acquired was timber-framed and the date over its main entrance was 1606. The Rothschilds built a larger house on the same site in the 19th century, and enlarged it again in the 20th century.

In 1949 Ascott House was presented to the National Trust. Architecturally the House is modest compared with other Trust properties. Indeed, the Trust's own Guide says: 'Ascott is one of the few country houses accepted by the Trust on other than architectural merits'.

But two other factors are important and establish Ascott's attraction. The first is the gardens. These, thirty acres in extent, were laid out at the end of the last century by that great Chelsea horticulturalist, Sir Harry Veitch. In part the gardens are formal, French style. But there are also many unusual trees and shrubs; there is a topiary sundial; and there are fine fountains with statuary. The most notable example is the work of the American sculptor, Ralph Waldo Story. From the gardens there are splendid views over the Vale of Aylesbury.

Ascott's other great claim lies in the contents of the house itself. There is French and English furniture of great quality. there are paintings by Rubens, Gainsborough, Hogarth, Hobbema and Turner. And there is also Anthony de Rothschild's magnificent collection of Chinese and Oriental porcelain. All in all, the treasures in Ascott House make it deservedly famous.

Halton House

This was the last Rothschild mansion to be built in Bucks – erected between 1882 and 1888. Alfred, who built it was an eccentric bachelor. He loved to drive about his estate in a carriage drawn by two zebras, and to conduct his own orchestra in his sumptuous Winter Garden.

During World War I the Halton estate became a great military camp. At any one time as many as 20,000 troops could be under training there. Alfred died in 1918 and the estate was then taken over permanently by the RAF. Between the two World Wars it became the central establishment for training all RAF apprentices in mechanical trades. Much has changed at Halton. The Winter Garden was demolished in 1935 to make way for other building more suitable to Halton's military use. But the great house itself remains, being used as the Officer's Mess.

Tring Park

Strictly, Tring is in Hertfordshire, not in Bucks. But it is only a mile or two from the border, and it has to be considered as part of the great Rothschild Squirearchy.

Baron Lionel Rothschild lived mostly in London, at Gunnersbury but he visited the Vale of Aylesbury frequently. He died in 1879. But before that he made sure that each of his three sons should inherit a country estate. With this in view in 1872 he purchased Tring Park with its four thousand acres of land for his eldest son, Nathaniel Meyer, who in 1885 became the first Lord Rothschild.

Nathaniel's son, Lionel, (1868–1937) became the second Lord Rothschild. His great passion was zoology. He set up the valuable Tring Museum of Natural History. Tring Park was sold after World War II and became a Girls' School. But the Rothschilds generously presented the Tring Museum of Natural History to the nation.

Chapter 7

Cards and Characters

One of the many dictionary definitions of a character is: 'a person represented in a play, film, story, etc., a role'. The hundred or more individuals we have been thinking of as 'figures in a Bucks Landscape' could also also be thought of as characters in that sense. All of them have been historical characters, playing their various roles in history seen in the setting of Bucks.

But a further dictionary definition of a 'character' is: 'an odd, eccentric, or unusual person'. as in the common phrase: 'He's quite a character'. Dickens provides good example of both these definitions. His novels are rich in characters of all kinds, each with a role to play in the story. But among them are some who definitely fit the second definition too. Thus, Sam Weller is a 'character', and so is Mr Pickwick.

But who or what is a 'card'? Again the dictionary can help us. It defines card in at least ten different ways. And one of them is: 'witty or eccentric person'. So a 'card' can be a character, but not all characters are cards!

To call a character a card is to use a slang word. Arnold Bennet wrote a whole novel about such a person. Indeed, he called his novel 'The Card'. And Dickens used 'card' in this way too. He writes of one character: '. . . his great aim was to be considered a *knowing* card'. And in 'Our Mutual Friend' he writes: 'You're a shaky old card, you can't be in love with this Lizzie'.

All of which opens the way for us to consider a few 'cards' or 'characters' in a Bucks context. All of them are odd or eccentric in one way or another. Of each of them you could say: 'He's quite a character', or, 'What a card he was'!

Francis Dashwood (1708–81)

He was wealthy. He was titled. He was an MP who held high office (Chancellor of the Exchequer, and Postmaster-General). And he was certainly a 'card'!

In the 1740s he became notorious as the founder of a secret society, The Knights of St. Francis of Wycombe, which became known as 'The Mad Monks of Medmenham'. The notoriety arose from the allegedly scandalous behaviour of the 'Monks' in the ruins of Medmenham Abbey. The 'Mad Monks' wore

West Wycombe Church with its golden globe.

white habits, but Dashwood, as the pseudo-St. Francis, sported a red bonnet. Mock nuns, recruited from the ladies of pleasure in London, were brought down to entertain the 'monks'.

The company of 'monks' included many of rank and position, including Frederick, Prince of Wales, Hogarth the artists, John Wilkes, Lord Melcombe and the Earl of Sandwich. As a group they were known as The Hell Fire Club.

The Mad Monks of Medmenham flourished from 1745 to 1763. Such rakish behaviour was quite a feature of 18th century social life for many. It may be that stories of Medmenham orgies were exaggerated, but there is no denying that Francis Dashwood and his cronies were cards and characters!

Yet it is also true that Dashwood was a conscientious landowner as well. He succeeded to the title of 15th Baron le Despencer in 1762. For thirty years he worked to rebuild West Wycombe house, to fill it with works of art, and to develop its magnificent grounds.

He also largely rebuilt West Wycombe Church, though here his eccentricity is evidenced in the famous golden ball which tops the steeple. It is big enough to accommodate three or four people at a time. John Wilkes boasted that he once attended a drinks party inside the golden ball. 'The best Globe Tavern I ever was in,' he boasted.

Sporting Parsons

One such was the Rector of Simpson, always known as Tally Ho! Hanmer. He was addicted to hunting and dressed accordingly. He sported mahogany-coloured top boots, a square-cut riding coat, with black breeches, crowned by a peculiar black hat with a broad flat brim.

He was constantly in debt, and spent quite a time in a Debtors' Prison. He sponged shamelessly on his friends and neighbours, and he loved to go up to London to dine and to attend the theatre.

Yet for all that, he was popular in his parish, charitable to the poor, and could preach excellent sermons. J. K. Fowler wrote of him:

*'His Rectory was generally barricaded against creditors
throughout the week. Only on Sundays could he walk
about in its grounds and visit his parishioners. Tally
Ho! Hanmer was a rollicking jolly sportsman, a
bachelor, of a type of class once very prevalent in
England. For good or ill such men are no more.'*

A second sporting parson was Loraine Smith of Passenham.
His great enthusiasm was Prize-fighting. For more about him,
see page 72. And mention of three other Men of the Cloth, who
were also in their different ways 'cards' or characters is made in
Chapter 5. They were Richard Carpenter, John Mason and
Newman Guest.

The Dinton Hermit

The Lord of the Manor of Dinton Hall near Aylesbury in the
17th century was Simon Mayne, friend and supporter of Oliver
Cromwell. Simon Mayne employed as Secretary and right-hand
man the learned and efficient John Bigg.

*The Dinton
Hermit, the
Inn Sign at
Ford. (NK)*

When the Civil War ended, with the execution of Charles I, Oliver Cromwell ruled the country for eleven years as Lord Protector. After his death the demand for the Restoration of the Monarchy was irresistible, and in 1660 Charles II returned from exile in France to ascend his executed father's throne. At once the hunt was on for the regicides who had signed the Death Warrant for Charles I.

All this was too much for the able and learned John Bigg. His mind became unhinged. For years he existed in the fields and hedgerows as a hermit. He lived off the food he could beg and on the wild fruits of the countryside. His appearance became more and more unkempt. He became famous for his extraordinary boots, patched and repatched year after year. (One of the boots is in the Ashmolean Museum in Oxford.)

Eventually he died and his grave is unknown. But he has a memorial of sorts – the village pub at Ford near Dinton Hall is named the Dinton Hermit.

One other fascinating facet of the life and death of this strange character is that some have alleged that John Bigg was the anonymous executioner who cut off King Charles I's head in Whitehall in 1649.

The Generous Miser

In 1814 the High Sheriff of Bucks died. His name was Nield. His wealth was inherited by his son, John Camden Nield. The inheritance included much landed property in Bucks, and also the patronage of the parish of North Marston.

John Camden Nield was a barrister who lived in lodgings with a housekeeper in Cheyne Walk, Chelsea. He was not just a character – he was a very miserly one. At regular intervals he journeyed into Bucks to collect his rents and tithes. He would always sit on the 'knifeboard' of the coach, this being the cheapest seat. One who knew him well described his appearance: 'His dress consisted of tight pantaloons, very much worn at the knees, Hessian boots, a threadbare blue coat with brass buttons, dirty buff waistcoat, high shirt collar, and a much-worn old low-crowned beaver hat'.

As he walked from one property to another he would eat a roll and boiled eggs, to save the cost of breakfasting at an inn. Sometimes he would sleep in a church porch, to save the cost of accommodation. He once surprised everybody by promising a subscription of £300 to the Bucks Infirmary – but he never paid it!

When Camden Nield died his Will caused a sensation. He left large landed estates in Bucks to Queen Victoria! He also left the Queen £250,000 in cash! Her Majesty sold the properties. She also found a very good use for the cash – she used it to purchase the Balmoral estate in Scotland!

The Queen acknowledged Nield's generous benefaction. She restored the Chancel of North Marston Church and erected there a new east window in Nield's memory. Beneath the floor of the chancel the eccentric miser is buried. And as a further gesture of the Queen's gratitude, she personally paid the £300 Nield had promised as a donation to the Bucks Infirmary but had never paid.

Loosely Speaking
William Loosley was a competent local builder whom Disraeli employed from time to time at Hughenden. In 1871 he claimed to have had a most extraordinary experience – he saw a U.F.O.! That term, meaning Unidentified Flying Object, hadn't been invented then. Nevertheless to Loosley the experience was very real. He gave a detailed report of it, which he called: 'An Account of a Meeting with Denizens of Another World'.

According to Loosley the incident happened on the night of October 4th, 1871. Unable to sleep, he was standing in his garden at midnight and he saw what he took to be a shooting star. But when he looked more closely he saw that it was moving with slow deliberation in a 'wandering, questing fashion'. He described how this 'thing' settled over Plummers Green and then came down to earth.

Next day he went searching for whatever it was that seemed to have come down to earth. In the bushes, he claims, he came across a metal-cased craft which 'moved with whirrings and lurchings'. There was a strange white globe suspended in the air above this mysterious craft. And there were hoops with globes at their centre, appearing and disappearing.

Loosley died in 1893 and is buried in Wycombe Cemetery. Did anyone believe him, or did they just dismiss him as a crank and a card? When he recounted that odd experience, was Loosley speaking truth, or was it rather a case of loosely speaking?

The Mad Hatter
Roger Crabbe of Chesham fought in the Civil War, suffering severe head wounds. At one point he was accused of indiscipline and was sentenced to death by Cromwell himself. But he was pardoned.

Having left the Army, Crabbe opened a hat shop in Chesham. He was deeply religious in an odd sort of way and almost starved himself to death. He dressed in sackcloth, ate nothing but bran and turnip-tops, and gave away all his money to the poor. His autobiography explains how his diet and his style of clothing enabled him to 'live on three-farthings a week'.

Gooseberry
An agnostic lady in Passenham asked that when she died a gooseberry should be buried with her. She explained that, if there *is* a God, a gooseberry bush would spring from her grave. Her wish was complied with. And for the record it has to be reported that a gooseberry bush *did* appear;.

'God Bless Your Majesty'
The loyal but dissenting pastor, John Heywood, was Pastor of the Independent Chapel of Potterspury. He was a 'larger than life' sort of figure. He was a familiar figure riding his grey horse. The long ends of his white cravat flapped in the wind and his waistcoat was invariably unbuttoned. People admired his eccentricities and respected his love of literature. They found him a man of simple heart and great cheerfulness. It was not only the villagers who knew and respected him. The Duke

of Grafton would often call on him, and Earl Temple often invited him to Stowe.

His greatest moment came when he went up to London soon after George III ascended the throne. The dissenting ministers went up to the throne to offer an Address of Congratulation. Mr Heywood went too, and was recognised by Earl Temple, remaining in conversation while the Address was presented. Heywood's chat with Earl Temple nearly distracted him from achieving the object of his journey to London. Looking up, he saw that His Majesty was about to conclude the Audience. Abruptly taking his leave from Earl Temple, Heywood called aloud, 'Stop, please your Majesty, stop! I have come all the way from Potterspury to kiss your Majesty's hand and I hope I shall be allowed the honour'. The King paused, and turned towards John Heywood, presenting his hand. John Heywood gave it two or three hearty kisses, adding: 'God Bless Your Majesty, and I hope you will make a good King'.

Chapter 8

Leading Ladies

Clearly the queen, wife, or consort of the monarch is a leading lady on any terms. Uniquely, Henry VIII had not one, but no less than six such consorts. Not all had special relevance in a Bucks context, but some did.

Catherine of Aragon

She was the daughter of Ferdinand of Aragon and Isabella of Castile. Even as an infant she was a key figure in the hopes of cementing more firmly the alliance between the England of Henry VII and the royal house of Spain. When she was only three Catherine was betrothed to Arthur, Prince of Wales, who was two.

In 1501, shortly before her 16th birthday, Catherine came to England. A few weeks later she and Arthur, who was fourteen, were married in Old St. Paul's. Arthur's younger brother, Henry, accompanied them up the aisle.

As part of her dowry Henry VII conferred on Catherine a number of Manors. In Bucks, these included Wendover and Whaddon. Meanwhile there was one other Bucks link with Catherine of Aragon – it is always attributed to her that she did much to promote what became a great Bucks industry – the making of lace for which Bucks became famous. As late as the 19th century lace-makers in Aylesbury annually celebrated 'Catterns Day' in her honour.

Within six months of the wedding of Arthur, the young bridegroom, was dead. Catherine always maintained that their marriage had never been consummated. Arthur's death meant that the alliance between England and Spain needed to be reconstructed. A solution lay ready to hand – Catherine could be married to Arthur's younger brother, Henry!

Catherine was now seventeen, but Henry was still only twelve, and for the moment at least unenthusiastic. Authority was successfully sought from the Pope that the marriage in due time could go ahead.

Henry VII died in 1509, and this made the marriage of his younger son the more urgent. That marriage took place in 1509. The prime requirement was the birth of a son who could one day succeed Henry VIII.

Catherine did her best! But she twice miscarried. Once she was delivered of a still-born daughter. Two boys were born but they died in infancy. Only one child survived – Princess Mary.

So Henry remained frustrated. He too had done his best! What he most desired, a healthy son to ensure the succession, had not been achieved. By 1627 Catherine at forty-two was assumed to be past further child-bearing. But Henry himself, at thirty-six, was still in his physical prime. In these circumstances, the 'King's great matter' was the subject of great discussion, both among the general public, and in the context of government and church debate.

By 1527 also Henry had fallen victim to the charms of Anne Boleyn. She would become the second consort of the monarch with Bucks connections. Three weeks after her fiftieth birthday, Catherine of Aragon died at Kimbolton Castle. She was buried in Peterborough Abbey, but Henry did not attend the funeral.

Anne Boleyn

Reduced to the barest facts, her history is that she was born in 1520, was married to Henry in 1532, and was executed by him in 1536.

She was described by some as 'the fair maid of Aylesbury'. This is because her father, Thomas Bullen, the Earl of Wiltshire, was also Lord of the Manor of Aylesbury. Before her marriage Anne lived at the Manor House in Aylesbury.

Anne Bolyen, 'the fair maid of Aylesbury'.

As 'the king's great matter' was being increasingly discussed, Anne began to be honoured at Court. By 1532 she was raised to the peerage in her own right as Marchioness of Pembroke. Cardinal Wolsey supported Henry's divorce from Catherine of Aragon. And Cranmer, who had become Archbishop of Canterbury, pronounced that Henry's first marriage, to Catherine, was void and that therefore he was free to marry Anne.

The marriage took place in 1532. In 1533 their first child was born, a daughter, Elizabeth. Later, in 1536, a few weeks after Catherine died, Anne miscarried. Ironically, that miscarried child was a boy.

Frustrated once more. Henry accused Anne of infidelity and sent her to the Tower. On 19th May, 1536, she was executed.

Henry's third wife, Jane Seymour, the only one of the six who bore him a son, had no connection with Bucks. Nor did his fourth wife, Anne of Cleeves. His fifth wife, Catherine Howard, did have a Bucks connection of sorts. She was Anne Boleyn's cousin, and was only nineteen when she was married to the fifty-year-old king. Accusations began to be levelled at the young queen – that she was guilty of adultery. Cranmer felt obliged to bring these accusations to the attention of the king. The most serious of the charges related to infidelities at Chenies in Bucks, with her cousin, Thomas Culpepper. Catherine went the way of her cousin, Anne Boleyn. She was tried and condemned and on 13 February 1542 she was beheaded at the Tower of London. Thomas Culpepper was also executed.

Henry's sixth and last wife was Catherine Parr. Her connection with Bucks is residential – at one stage of her life she lived at Beachampton House. She had already been widowed twice when, aged thirty-one, she married Henry in 1543. Henry, then fifty-two, was largely an invalid. Catherine was a dutiful nurse to him rather than a wife.

But there are other notable women who can fairly be described as 'leading ladies' besides the wives and consorts of monarchs. Two such are closely connected with Claydon. The first of these was:

Lady Verney

When Sir Edmund Verney of Claydon was killed at the king's side in the Battle of Edgehill in 1642, he was succeeded by his son, Sir Ralph Verney. Sir Ralph was a keen supporter of the Parliamentary cause. But there was a snag. The victorious Roundheads demanded that all their supporters should sign a Covenant which would abolish episcopacy and enforce presbyterianism as the national form of religion in England. This, in conscience, Sir Ralph could not do. It was made clear that his estate would be in the gravest danger of sequestration if he did not comply.

This was a bitter irony. Sir Ralph, a Member of Parliament whose only wish had been to see Parliament triumph against the king, found himself now in a great crisis. He decided that he must go into exile. He fled to France in 1643. Before leaving he did what he could to protect his house and estates at Claydon. He left them in the hands of Trustees. And his wife, Lady Verney, remained in England to protect their interests.

The plan didn't work. A flaw in one of the Trust Deeds led to the Claydon lands being sequestered any way. By then Sir Ralph was out of the country and could only hope that his wife would be able to get the sequestration order lifted.

What followed was a lengthy, titanic struggle – a struggle waged by Lady Verney already suffering from the cancer which would later kill her. The Verney finances were already burdened by debt. Sir Ralph had succeeded to an estate worth £2,000 a year, but he also inherited debts totaling £11,000. Just to pay the interest charges alone imposed a fearful burden, and made it all the more urgent to get the sequestration order lifted.

In theory there was, ready to hand, a way of escape. Owners could retain, or regain, their lands on payment of fines commensurate with the yearly value of the property. But they could only follow this path – the process was called 'Composition' – if they first swore allegiance to Parliament's religious settlement. And this Sir Ralph steadfastly declined to do.

Sir Ralph remained in exile in France for five years, while the brave Lady Verney kept up the fight at home. Parliament next brought a new weapon to bear against Sir Ralph. He was a member of Parliament, and because he was now an absentee Member, this fact was said to compound his delinquency.

But even if Sir Ralph surrendered, and returned to England to plead his own case, he felt unable to do so. He knew that the moment he set foot in England he would be arrested for debt. So he stayed abroad, and the brave, ailing Lady Verney carried on the struggle.

Income from sequestered property was collected by Local Country Committees. All her efforts to deal with the Local Committee in Bucks had been unavailing. She decided she must take her case to Parliament itself, by-passing the Local Committee. Time after time her attempts to do so were frustrated.

She wrote a desperate letter to her husband:

'I cannot imagine what course to take, for everybody tells me that there is no hope of doing anything in the Commons but by bribery, and where shall we get the money I vow I know not.'

Against all the odds, she did succeed at last in getting their case before the Committee. On January 5th, 1648, the voting went eleven to three in favour of the Verneys.

Once that had happened, Sir Ralph began to prepare to return to England. With sequestration lifted, there still

Claydon House for which Lady Verney fought so hard. (NK)

remained the enormous task of tackling the debts. For this, lands had to be sold, and deals had to be struck to cajole creditors into accepting a reduction in accumulated interest. The Verney finances would be straitened for a long time to come. For many families, similarly placed, such struggles ended in failure and some Manors and Lordships disappeared forever. That this did not happen to the Verneys is a temendous tribute to the courage and tenacity of Lady Verney, dying as she was from cancer. Today, three centuries later, there are still Verneys at Claydon.

At the Restoration, with Charles II on the throne, Sir Ralph successfully petitioned the monarch for a baronetcy in recompense for the wrongs and ills he had suffered at the hands of Parliament. So here was a second irony. Sir Ralph had opposed Charles I and had thrown his weight on Parliament's side. Now, eleven years later, he successfully sought redress from Charles II against the Parliament that had treated him so harshly.

The Lady with the Lamp

The second 'leading lady' associated with Claydon was Florence Nightingale. Her sister, Parthenope, had married Sir Harry Verney. Florence was a frequent visitor to their home at Claydon. The two girls were the daughters of William and Fanny Nightingale. Both daughters were born in Italy, in which country the family often travelled. Both daughters were named after the places where they happened to be born. William taught both his daughters himself. Both were clever, amiable dilettanti, fluent in Italian, French, Latin and Greek.

Florence was born (in the city of that name) on May 12th, 1820. Her sister, Parthenope married Sir Harry Verney, but Florence, declining several offers of marriage, remained unwed and devoted her life to nursing. As the world knows, she found deserved fame for her heroic work of nursing in the Crimean War, earning the nickname by which she will ever be known – The Lady with the Lamp.

But the Crimean War was by no means the end of her career or her fame. She returned to England in 1856 and set up the first institution in England for training nurses, at St. Thomas and Kings College Hospitals in London.

She lived to the ripe old age of ninety, dying in 1910. To the

Florence Nightingale, the Lady with the Lamp.

very end she was active, constantly consulted on all health matters. Her stays at Claydon were lengthy. Two rooms there are in effect a Nightingale Museum, full of memorabilia connected with her long and astonishing career.

Great Political Hostesses

The important role played by Hester Temple at Stowe has already been related (see page 39). She was the wife of Richard Grenville and the mother of one Prime Minister, George Grenville, the mother-in-law of another, William Pitt, and the grandmother of a third, Pitt the Younger. Altogether, then, a leading lady of consequence.

It is interesting to compare one great political hostess with another, and to turn from one great country house to a second. So from Hester Temple at Stowe, we turn to Lady Nancy and Cliveden.

Nancy Astor (1879–1964) was the American-born British politician born in Virginia. She married William Astor, the 2nd Viscount Astor, the English politician who was the son of the American-born British newspaper proprietor, William Waldorf Astor, who had been made 1st Viscount Astor.

The 2nd Viscount Astor was elected to Parliament in 1910 as MP for Plymouth. On his elevation to the House of Lords, his wife succeeded him as MP for Plymouth. Nancy Astor thereby became the first woman ever to take her seat in the House of Commons.

Their home was Cliveden, the third house to be built on that Thames-side site. In the 1930s the house became the meeting place of what became known as 'the Cliveden Set'. This was a loose grouping of politicians and celebrities whose chief interest was the avoidance of the war with Germany which in the thirties was threatening. Though many criticized the 'Cliveden Set' as being too ready to appease Hitler, others recognised that their efforts were simply to avert war.

Cliveden came into the news again in 1963 when it was the setting for what became known as 'the Profumo Affair'. In 1942 Cliveden was given to the National Trust, though members of the Astor family still lived there till 1966. Today, still owned by the National Trust, it is run as a privately-managed luxury hotel.

Murdered by the Butcher

At the end of the 17th century Mrs Bennet was the wealthy widow of the Lord of the Manor of Calverton. She lived in a perpetual state of feud with her neighbours and tenants, and conducted a running dispute with the Rector over the payment of tithes.

It was common knowledge that she kept lots of money in the Manor House, as Cole, the Bletchley diarist, noted: '. . . being of a miserable disposition she lived by herself in the old house at Calverton . . . A butcher of Stony Stratford artfully got into the house, and there being nobody to assist her, or call for help, he barbarously murdered her, circa 1691, for which he was afterwards executed'. The murder took place on the night of Stony Stratford's Horse and Hiring Fair.

Leading Ladies in Glass

All Saints Church in High Wycombe has a modern stained-glass window which is exclusively dedicated to leading ladies. They cover many centuries and many walks of life. All are women famed for their service to others. They are: Queen Victoria, Grace Darling, Emily Bronte, Mary Slessor, Christina Rosetti, Elizabeth Fry, Florence Nightingale, Margaret Godolphin, Margaret Roper, Margaret Beaufort, Alice Marvel. And the Saints: Bridget, Frideswide, Margaret and Winefred.

Catherine Browne Willis

She was a person of noble descent and could trace her ancestry all the way back to Walter Giffard, the first Earl of Buckingham, in the time of William the Conqueror. She died in 1724, aged only thirty-four. She had been married seventeen years and she bore no less than ten children. And she was an author. Her first book, published in 1717, was called 'The Whole Duty of Man'. A year later, in 1718, she published a second book, called 'The Established Church of England'.

It has to be said that Browne Willis poured scorn on his wife's books, and made them the subject of continual mockery. Yet his own books (and he wrote at least a dozen between 1715 and 1756) did not escape criticism. Apart from his 'History of Buckingham' none of his other books could be described as 'a good read'. One critic said of them: 'It is as if he has published the Indexes and left out the books'.

For Catherine, to have borne ten children and also to have published at least two books before dying at the age of thirty-four, not to mention seventeen years of marriage to an eccentric and often cantankerous husband, she surely deserves to be included in this catalogue of leading ladies.

To end this catalogue of leading ladies who have been prominent in Bucks history perhaps, as a sort of post-script, we should acknowledge that the term 'leading lady' also has

Fay Compton's cottage near Bletchley. (NK)

theatrical connotations. At least one theatrical leading lady has a Bucks connection. She was Fay Compton (1894–1978). She owned a tiny cottage by the side of the road that runs from Bletchley to Buckingham. She loved to escape to it and to enjoy the peace and quiet of the Bucks countryside after her West-End successes.

Chapter 9

Plotters, Regicides and Antiheroes

The Gunpowder Plot

In the very north of Bucks, about three miles from each other,
stand the two great houses of Gayhurst and Tyringham.
Between them flows the Great Ouse. Both have connections
with the Gunpowder Plot of 1605, one house directly, the other
indirectly. Tyringham's connection with the Plot is indirect,
arising only from the fact that one of the conspirators was
connected by marriage to the Tyringham family. He was Robert
Catesby, a member of the wealthy Catesby family whose seat
was at Ashby St. Legers in Northants.

Across the river at Gayhurst was Everard Digby. He was
young, active and intelligent – the sort of man of whom it could
be said that 'he had everything going for him'. He had acquired
Gayhurst Manor by marriage, having in 1581 married Mary
Mulsho, the daughter of William Mulsho, the Lord of the
Manor of Gayhurst. William had begun the work of building
the new Gayhurst Manor by extending the Elizabethan house
which already existed. When Everard Digby married Mary he
continued the building of the great new house started by his
late father-in-law.

Robert Catesby and Everard Digby had two things in
common – they were friends and they were Catholics. When-
ever Catesby, from Ashby St. Legers visited his kinsfolk-by-
marriage at Tyringham, he could cross the Ouse and visit his
friend at Gayhurst, a short three miles away.

When the young Digby took on the work of building the
new Gayhurst from his late father-in-law, he had every

Gayhurst Manor. (NK)

opportunity as a Catholic to include in the building secret
passages, a priest's hiding place, and a discreet small chapel
where Mass could be said.

Ever since the Reformation Catholics had experienced every
kind of emotion. They had rejoiced when Mary became Queen
in 1553 and restored the Roman Catholic faith in England; they
had been perplexed and bemused during the reign of Elizabeth,
when that monarch sought to fashion a middle way; they had
been proscribed and forbidden to practice their religion, and
their priests were constantly harried.

Elizabeth died in 1603 and was succeeded by James I
(James VI of Scotland). The question then was – how would
religion fare under the new king? Two opposite factions hoped
that he would favour them, the Puritans and the Catholics. Or
would he persist in following the medium way initiated by
Elizabeth?

Digby was one of those knighted by the new king, but he
soon began to despair of any concessions being granted to
Catholics. This, then, is the context in which the plotting to

remove the king began. Some of that plotting was done in the Gate House at the entry to Ashby St.. Legers. And some of it was done at Gayhurst. Meeting there were Guy Fawkes, Robert Catesby and Everard Digby. As well as playing host to the plotters at Gayhurst, Everard Digby also contributed £1,500 towards the cost of the plot, selling some land to raise the money.

In barest outline, the plot was to blow up Parliament, removing in one big bang both the Royal Family and the Commons, and then immediately to seek to foster a Catholic uprising in the country.

But in the night of November 5th, 1605, the plot failed on both counts. Guy Fawkes was caught red-handed in the cellar beneath Parliament; Digby, whose special role should have been to have raised the Catholic uprising in the west country, was obliged to surrender and was subsequently beheaded. Guy Fawkes met the same fate. And Catesby was shot while resisting arrest.

The Double Plot

James I escaped death when the Gunpowder Plot of 1605 failed. But he had been in peril twice over, two years before that. Because Elizabeth was unmarried and childless, the question of a successor when she died had exercised many minds. Though it was expected that her cousin, James VI of Scotland would become James I of England, there were some determined to prevent this.

Two plots were hatched at about the same time. In July 1603 what became known as the BYE PLOT was hatched by Thomas, Lord Grey de Wilton of Bletchley with certain others. It was a fairly unsophisticated plot – simply to seize the new king, and to try to force him as a prisoner to agree to grant religious toleration.

Simultaneously there was also what was known as THE MAIN PLOT. This was a more complicated affair whose aim was to depose James I and in his place to put the young Arabella Stuart on the throne. The plotters in this instance were Sir Walter Raleigh, Lord Cobham, and once again, Lord Grey de Wilton of Bletchley.

Both plots failed even before they could really be started. Many arrests were made and executions followed. The three principal plotters were reprieved. But they did not go unpunished. Lord Grey of Bletchley was sent to the Tower and spent the remaining eleven years of his life a prisoner there. He died in the Tower in 1614.

Meanwhile all his estates had been forfeited to the crown. In 1616 the king made a gift to his favourite, George Villiers, of the Manors of Water Eaton, Bletchley and Fenny Stratford. Thus came to an end the power of the Greys in North Bucks. For fifteen generations covering some four or five centuries they had held sway. It all ended in the failure of The Bye Plot and the main Plot in 1603.

The Waller Plot

Edmund Waller (1606–87) was a cousin of John Hampden. He married an heiress and was a Member of Parliament. His home was at Hall Barns near Beaconsfield, and he was a considerable poet.

As the relationship between Charles I and Parliament deteriorated it was inevitable that a civil war would ensue. Waller's sympathies were for the king. He recognised the importance of London to the king, but the king was out of the capital and with his army in the country. Waller's plot in May 1643 was aimed at betraying London to the king. But Waller himself betrayed the plot through his own inefficiency. He was expelled from the House of Commons and sent to gaol, and then sentenced to banishment. But Cromwell relented and in 1650 permitted Waller to return to this country. Waller then became an enthusiastic supporter of the Roundhead cause! (But for more details of his Janus-like behaviour, see page 52.)

James II Abdicates

The Rye House Plot of 1683 was aimed at getting rid of both Charles II and his brother, the future James II. The plot failed. But pressure was kept up on James II and in 1688 he abdicated. This made possible the joint monarchy of William and Mary.

(Mary was the sister of James, but did not share his desire to restore the Catholic faith in England.)

With the Stuart king, James II, an exile in France, there were some attempts to plot on behalf of the Stuarts and to secure their restoration. Such attempts were described as Jacobite – Jacobus being the Latin form of the name James.

One enthusiast for this cause was Francis Atterbury. he had been born in 1663 in the village of Milton Keynes where his father was Vicar. Francis too went into the ministry and quickly found preferrment. He went from being Dean of Carlisle to the Deanery of Christ Church, and then became Bishop of Rochester and Dean of Westminster. By then the year was 1713. In 1714 Queen Anne, the last of the Stuarts, died. She was succeeded by George, the first of the Hanover dynasty.

The new king required all Bishops to make a declaration of fidelity. Francis Atterbury declined. He was accused of plotting to try to bring back the Stuarts and was committed to the Tower. In 1722 a Bill of Pains and Penalties was passed, depriving Atterbury of all his offices. More than that, he was banished from the kingdom. So in 1723 he left England and his last years were spent in exile. After his death in 1732 his body was brought back to England and buried in an unnamed grave in Westminster Abbey.

The Regicides

In January 1649 Commons appointed a High Court of Justice to try the defeated Charles I. The Court sat in Westminster Hall for ten days and passed sentence of death on him. Cromwell himself was one of the fifty-nine members who signed the Death Warrant. These fifty-nine are the Regicides. Some eight or nine of them were from Bucks.

Robert Hammond

He was a Colonel in the Roundhead Army and was Cromwell's cousin. He was made Governor of the Isle of Wight where Charles was held prisoner in Carisbrooke Castle until his trial. Later, Hammond acquired the Manor of Willen (now part of

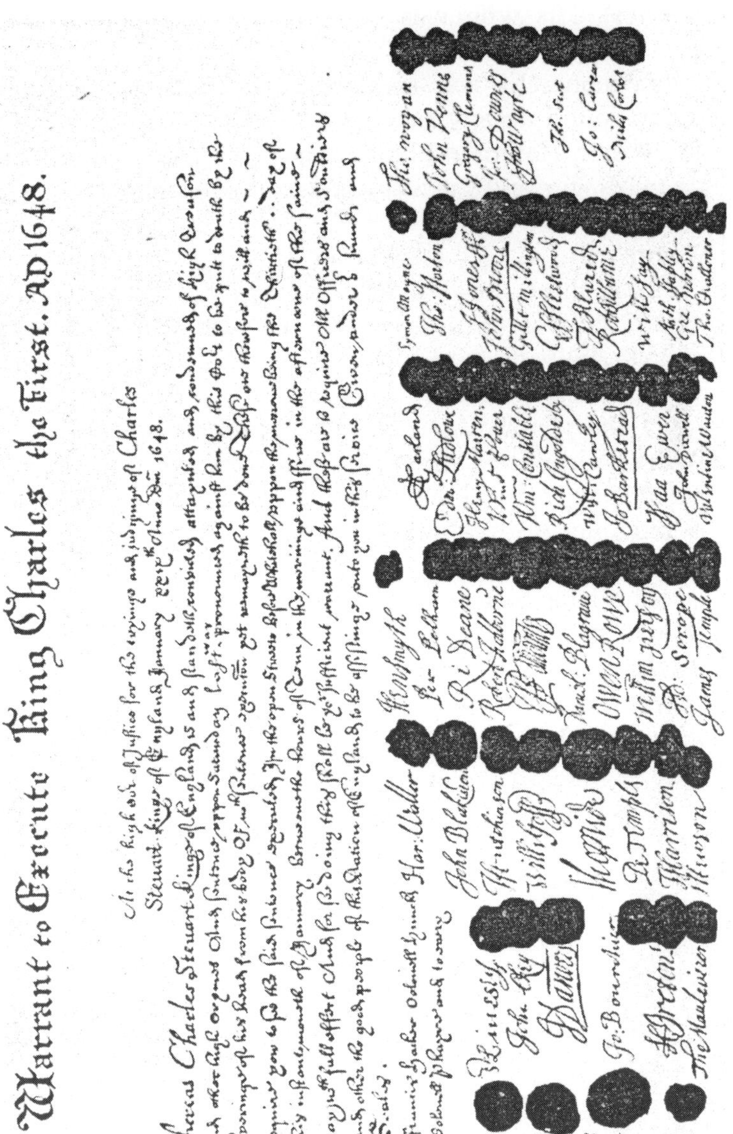

Warrant to Execute King Charles the First. AD 1648.

At the high Court of Justice for the tryinge and judginge of Charles Steuart Kinge of England January xxix Anno Dni 1648.

Death Warrant for Charles I

Milton Keynes). His wife was one of John Hampden's six daughters.

When the monarchy was restored in 1660 great attempts were made to round up any surviving regicides and to punish them. But by then Hammond had already died. In his will he left Willen to his wife and she was not deprived of it.

Simon Mayne

On the 14th of June, 1645, the Battle of Naseby virtually brought the Civil war to an end. The defeated Charles I left behind him on the battlefield some eight hundred dead, 4,500 prisoners, and all his artillery.

Next day the victorious Cromwell stayed at Dinton Hall with his friend supporter, Simon Mayne. Mayne had been a whole-hearted supporter of the Parliamentary cause. In 1642 he had presented an Address to the King, calling on him to disband the army.

Seven years later Mayne was present in Westminster Hall for the whole of the King's trial. And he was one of the fifty-nine who signed the Death Warrant. After the restoration of the monarchy in 1660 Mayne was arrested and imprisoned in

Dinton Hall, home of Simon Mayne. (JH)

the Tower. He was put on trial at the Old Bailey and sentenced to death. But he was already a broken man and he died in prison before he could be executed. His body was taken to Dinton and he is buried in the church there. (For the extraordinary story of Mayne's secretary, 'the Dinton Hermit', see page 92.)

Richard Deane

He was from Princes Risborough and was an active supporter of Cromwell under whom he rose to high office. At the King's trial he was one of the fifty-nine regicides who signed the Death Warrant in 1649. In 1653 he lost his life in a naval action off the North Foreland. He was given a State Funeral in Westminster Abbey.

When the regicides were being hunted down after the restoration of the monarchy, Deane had already been dead seven years. So he could not be brought to trial. But orders were given that his remains should be disinterred and removed from the Abbey.

Sir Richard Ingoldsby

He was Lord of the Manor of Waldridge and so was a neighbour of Simon Mayne of Dinton Hall. He was MP for Aylesbury for four Parliaments. In the Civil War he served in the Roundhead Army and he was member of the High Court of Justice to try the king. His was one of the fifty-nine regicides on the Death Warrant.

It was claimed afterwards that though he was a member of the High Court of Justice, he never actually attended during the Trial. How, then, did he come to sign the Death Warrant? The explanation offered was that Cromwell personally had seized Ingoldsby's hand and pen and physically forced him against his will to append his signature.

Ingoldsby was a survivor! He later entered into negotiations with the agents of Charles II and through them made his peace with the king. So, at the Coronation of Charles II, Ingoldsby was there! Despite that signature on the Death Warrant of his father, Charles II made Ingoldsby a KCB! He survived till 1685, leaving behind him seven grandsons and seven grand-daughters.

Some Antiheroes

'A central character in a novel, play, etc., who lacks the traditional heroic virtues". Such is the dictionary definition of an antihero. So who might figure in the Bucks Landscape answering such a description? One example may very well be:

Judge Jeffreys (1648–89)

This English Judge was born near Wrexham, but in 1686 he bought Bulstrode Park near Gerrards Cross. He completely rebuilt the house and later left it to his daughter and her husband.

Called to the bar in 1668, he rose rapidly in his profession. He became Chief Justice of Chester and went on in 1683 to be Chief Justice of Kings Bench. By inclination he was a Puritan, but he was ambitious too, and assiduously courted royal favour. He was made Solicitor to the Duke of York and was knighted in 1677. He earned the favour of James II who raised him to the peerage.

Thus far, his record does not suggest too many anti-heroic characteristics. But the fact is that Jeffreys could be said to have operated at two different levels. In civil cases he was an able and impartial lawyer and judge. But in criminal cases he could be, and often was, ruthless and sadistic. This was particularly evident when he was trying cases where his decisions and sentences might influence the king's opinion of him.

Two of his earliest trials were those of Titus Oates and Richard Baxter. Both were of Protestant religion and therefore opponents of the Catholic-minded James II. Jeffreys was very brutal in his treatment of them both.

But his notoriety is particularly based on his conduct when he went to the west country to try the followers of the Duke of Monmouth. The Duke was an illegitimate son of Charles II. In 1685 he attempted a rebellion which, he hoped, would gain him

PLOTTERS, REGICIDES
AND ANTIHEROES

the throne and expel James II. The rebellion ended in his comprehensive defeat at the Battle of Sedgemoor. Monmouth was executed on Tower Hill in 1685.

Meanwhile many of his followers were arraigned before Judge Jeffreys who, in what became known as 'The Bloody Assizes', hanged, transported, whipped and fined hundreds of them.

But three years later King James II himself, whose favour Jeffreys had tried so hard to gain, fell from power. He abdicated and fled to France.

The hated Jeffreys was then in mortal danger. He went into hiding and then, disguised as a sailor, he tried to escape to France. But he was caught napping at Wapping! The mob might well have lynched him had he not been sent to the Tower for his own safety. And in the Tower he died.

Sir Oswald Mosley (1896–1980)
Just outside the village of Denham lies Savay Farm. Sir Oswald Mosley lived here. His wife died there and lies buried in the grounds beneath a monument designed by Lutyens.

As a politician Mosley graduated from being an Independent, then a Conservative, and then as a Labour MP. He was a Member of the 1929 Labour Government. Before the outbreak of World War II he became Leader of the British Union of Fascists – The Blackshirts. On the outbreak of war he was detained under the Defence Regulations. In 1948 he founded a new 'Union' Movement.

Robert Maxwell
Does he qualify as an antihero? He was born in Czechoslovakia in 1923 and served in the war (1940–45). After the war he founded the Pergamum Press and became extensively involved in the printing and publishing worlds.

He also went into politics and was Labour MP for Buckingham. When the new city of Milton Keynes was decided upon, Maxwell was one of two business tycoons shortlisted as likely chairmen of the Milton Keynes Development Corporation. In the event the appointment went to the other man, Lord Campbell of Eskham.

Maxwell was drowned at sea, falling from his luxury yacht. His death left enormous debts behind, including the loss of millions of pounds from the Pension Funds of his employees.

And One More Plot

This chapter began by recounting a few of the notable plots that have figured in Bucks history. Here is one other plot – of a quite different kind. It, too, was hatched in Bucks. And, as with Bob Maxwell, there is a connection both with the county and with Czechoslovakia.

In World War II the Abbey at Aston Abbotts was the home of the Czech President, Eduard Benes, and his Government in exile. Less than two miles away, at Wingrave, lived Jan Masaryk, the Czech Foreign Minister. It was at the Abbey at Aston Abbotts that these two men planned the assassination of

Wingrave Hall. Jan Masaryk, the exiled Czech Foreign Minister, lived here in World War II. (NK)

the Nazi Gestapo chief, Reinhard Heydrich. The plot, hatched in the peace of the Bucks countryside, was successfully carried out as Czech assassins executed the reviled Heydrich. But there was also a dreadful reprisal – Lidice Village was razed to the ground and every man there was put to death to revenge the death of Heydrich.

Chapter 10

'The Long March of Everyman'

Ecclesiasticus in the Bible bids us: *'Let us now praise famous men and our fathers that begat us'*. Centuries later Burke warned us: 'Men will never look forward to posterity who never look back to their ancestors'.

In our survey of many of the notable men and women who have been figures in our Bucks landscape, we have been following the injunctions of both Burke and Ecclesiasticus, But we should also notice how that passage from Ecclesiasticus goes on. He wrote:

> *'Let us also praise the common man. He puts his trust in his hands and becomes wise in his own work; without the common man the city cannot be inhabited. You may not find him in the Councils, and in the Assembly he may not mount up on high; he may not sit in the seat of the Judge, but the common man will maintain the fabric of the world.'*

Centuries later Disraeli once said: 'If the cottage is not happy the castle is not safe'.

It is right, then, that in this closing chapter we should consider 'the common man', who has figured down the centuries in our Bucks landscape. And whoever defined Social history as 'the long march of everyman' was surely right, and gives us a very apt title for this concluding chapter.

The Men at Arms, the Men of State, the Men of Wealth, and the Men of the Cloth were dominant in our county history. And the Men of Letters recorded their doings and painted word pictures of them. But far more numerous, and just as important have been the ordinary folk. They are the retainers who marched to war at their masters' command; the countrymen who ploughed the fields and tended the flocks; the labourers who helped built the manors and maintained the roads; the worshippers who sat at the feet of the priests and ministers in the churches.

They 'put their trust in their hands', and 'became wise in their own work'. Predominantly they were agricultural workers, for Bucks has always been an agricultural county. But they also include the women who made the lace for which Bucks became famous; and the folk who developed the extraordinary needle-making industry at Long Crendon; and the chair-makers of Wycombe; they are the grooms and ostlers who helped keep the coaches running on the Watling Street; and the makers of bricks, tiles and pots; the forestry workers, the tanners and brewers, and the brush-makers of Bletchley.

Needles

Perhaps the least expected of all of these are the needle-makers of Long Crendon. Needle-making began there in 1560 when Elizabeth was on the throne. It was started by Christopher Greening and it lasted till the reign of Queen Victoria. It was all hand-labour. It lost out inevitably to Redditch in Victorian times when a steam engine and modern machinery there made the 'cottage industry' of Long Crendon no longer tenable.

But in its hey day at Long Crendon, 'cottage industry' though it may have been, it produced in prodigious quantities an astonishing range of needles – for sail-making, tent-making, sewing and surgery. Lipscombe wrote in 1802 that more than a thousand people were engaged in the industry. The Shrimpton family was prominent. Old Thomas Shrimpton had sixteen children, eight boys and eight girls, and all were needle makers. At intervals, when enough needles of all kinds had been made, they were taken up to London for sale.

Lace

Whether or not Catherine of Aragon can really be credited with introducing lace-making to Bucks, it was certainly given a fillip by her. Olney and Newport Pagnell were great lace-making centres. It was said that more lace was produced at Newport Pagnell than anywhere else in the kingdom. And Catherine of Aragon lived for a while at Ampthill, just over the border.

Later, foreign lace-makers settled in the district also, and the art spread south to Aylesbury and to High Wycombe. It was entirely a cottage industry. Lace buyers made the round of the villages to buy up the lace produced in hundreds of cottages. In 1801, out of the 1,275 inhabitants of Hanslope, eight hundred were lace-makers.

The art was taught in special schools. As long ago as1626 Sir Henry Borlase founded a free school at Great Marlow for twenty-four boys and twenty-four girls to learn 'to knit, spin, and make lace'.

One of Cowper's poems describes the lace-making he saw going on in Olney and in virtually every other nearby village. Perhaps the last line of his poem is rather less than flattering:

> *'Yon cottager, who weaves at her own door*
> *Pillow and bobbin all her little store;*
> *Content though mean, and cheerful if not gay,*
> *Shuffling her threads about the livelong day,*
> *Just earns a scanty pittance; and at night*
> *Lies down secure, her heart and pocket light;*
> *She, for her humble sphere by nature fit,*
> *Has little understanding, and no wit.'*

Just as Long Crendon's needle-making was overtaken in Victorian times by the machine-made needles of Redditch, so too was Bucks lace-making overtaken by the machine-made lace of Nottingham.

Chairs

Chairs, especially Windsor chairs, have been made in Wycombe for two hundred and fifty years or more, using the woods of the area, including beech. Before the end of the 17th century wooden bedframes were being supplied to the London market.

In Victorian times there were fifty chair-makers in Wycombe. They used foot-operated lathes until the Industrial

Revolution introduced power-driven lathes. By 1870 the output of chairs was an astonishing five thousand a day. A mammoth order for chairs was placed in 1873, for 19,000 chairs for a Moody and Sankey evangelical meeting in London. Another order was for 8,000 chairs for the Crystal Palace, erected in Hyde Park for the Great Exhibition in 1851.

The beechwoods of South Bucks made possible the industries of wood-turning and furniture-making. Daniel Defoe commented in 1725 on the prodigious quantities of wood used for making spokes and rims for the wheels of carts and carriages.

Furniture-making drew still further on the beechwood resources. Much of the work was done in the beechwoods by individual workmen called 'bodgers'. They with their pole-lathes cut and turned chair legs to supply the factories in Wycombe where the chairs were produced in vast quantities.

In these and in other local industries men and women of Bucks 'put their trust in their hands', and 'became wise in their own work'. They had their chroniclers. The delightful books of Harman and J. K. Fowler describe such people, their works and ways, their doings and often their dialects. It is sad that the books are now out of print. For many who can find them, they are a delight.

Let one example suffice. It comes from J. K. Fowler's 'Recollections of old County Life'. He has been describing how, long ago, nearly every farmer, and many householders too, brewed their own beer. Beer brewed in October would be fit for consumption in January or February. The March brewing was fit to drink in the summer and autumn.

Good beer was thought to be of good strength if it was brewed with eight bushels to the hogshead of fifty-four gallons. Fowler goes on:

> 'At an outlying village in Bucks, the Rector on a certain Sunday, gave out as his text: HEBREWS 9 and 10, whereupon an old-fashioned farmer, renowned for a good tap, called out: "And wery pretty tipple too. I BREWS EIGHT". He explained to the Rector after church

*that he meant eight bushels to the hogshead. The
worthy Rector, to enable him to test the quality, called
on him a few days afterwards and pronounced the
brewing excellent, and explained his text more fully,
and, it is hoped, satisfactorily.'*

As well as their chroniclers, the 'ordinary folk' of Bucks
have their characters too. There was the redoubtable of
Charlotte Gregory, a famous lace-maker of Loughton. She
continued to sit at her lace-making well into her nineties. She
always smoked a clay pipe. When a sufficient amount of
nicotine collected in her mouth, she would remove her clay
pipe, and discharge the nicotine accumulation over a
considerable distance into the fire with unerring accuracy.
Witnesses came to witness the spectacle while pretending to
praise her lace.

Another spitter, this time nameless was the parishioner of
St. Martin's Church in Fenny Stratford. It was in 1880. The
Bishop of Oxford had just laid the Foundation Stone of an
extension to the church. As the assembled dignitaries politely
applauded, a parishioner among them spat on the stone! He
meant no disrespect, it was his way of wishing the extended
church good luck! But all present were scandalised and
embarrassed. Next day, church officials called on the man and
told him he must go in person to Oxford to apologise to the
Bishop. He did as he was told. A newspaper account of the
incident said that the man in this way 'penitentially expiated
his untimely expectoration'.

Another individual who brought down wrath upon himself
with far grimmer results was George Taylor of Newport
Pagnell. He was foolish enough to comment publicly on
Henry VIII and his matrimonial entanglements. George Taylor
said: 'The King is but a knave and liveth in adultery, and is a
heretic and liveth not after the laws of God. I set not by the
King's crown and if I had it here I would play football with it'.

That was in 1535. Those brave words caused George Taylor
to be charged at the Assizes at Little Brickhill. He was found
guilty and sentenced to be hanged.

To the left of the steep path up to Little Brickhill church door a prominent tomb houses the remains of a man with the remarkable name of True Blue. He had been an Officer's batman in the Royal Horse Guards – The Blues. He was rewarded for an act of heroism rather like that performed by William Ovitts of Winslow (see page 26).

In True Blue's case what happened was that his master had been taken prisoner in the wars. Blue managed to rescue him. In gratitude, his officer bought Blue's discharge from the Army. True Blue came to Little Brickhill and became the landlord of the White Lion Inn in the village. The prominent tomb on the church path is his memorial.

The Four Site Saga

Perhaps a good example of corporate heroism is seen in the successful struggle waged by hundreds of ordinary folk to prevent London's Third Airport from being built in North Bucks.

Wing was one of the hundreds of wartime airfields. In 1969 it was announced that it was proposed as the site for London's Third Airport. It would be called Cublington rather than Wing, Cublington being a nearby village. Consternation greeted the news. If the plan went ahead three whole villages would be obliterated – Cublington, Stewkley and Dunton. Two others, Soulbury and Whitchurch – might not escape either. But ironically Wing itself would survive.

Two thousand people would lose their homes and a further ten thousand would suffer the inevitable noise pollution. Stewkley Church, one of only three in the whole country with such perfect Norman dog-toothed carving, would disappear under a sea of concrete.

A great Campaign was energetically launched to fight the proposal. It enrolled over 65,000 members and raised over £60,000. The use made of publicity and the media was masterly. The fight went on for two whole years.

It transpired that the Cublington site was only one of four possible alternatives. The others were Nuthamstead, Thurleigh and Foulness (Maplin Sands). But Cublington seemed to be the most likely. So the fight to oppose it went on with renewed vigour. Several books have been written about it, including the aptly-named 'The Four Site Saga'.

And in the end the fight was won. Victory was signalled in 1971 when the Government announced that Cublington would *not* be the site of London's Third Airport. In the event, neither was any of the other three. It was after all Stanstead that had the 'honour'. Tens of thousands of people in North Bucks can only salute the tenacity of all those ordinary folk who fought so hard and so successfully to stop London's Third Airport from swallowing up Cublington, Dunton and Stewkley. To mark this great environmental victory four hundred trees were planted in 1972 with this inscription:

CUBLINGTON SPINNEY

This spinney was planted in 1972 by the Buckinghamshire County Council in gratitude to all those who supported the campaign against the recommendation that London's Third Airport should be at Cublington. Parish Councils, organisations, societies and many individuals contributed towards the cost of the Spinney. This point is the centre of the area proposed for the Airport.

Mid-most unmitigated England.

Chapter 11

The Code Breakers
of Bletchley Park

The preceding ten chapters of this book have touched on more than a hundred notable men and women who have been historic figures in the Buckinghamshire landscape. They have ranged over the centuries from the first to the twentieth. Their notability has stretched from military importance to literary genius . . . from ecclesiastical fame to aesthetic enthusiasm . . from eccentricity to 'ordinariness' often manifested in extra-ordinary ways.

We come now to a very special class of historic figures in the Buckinghamshire landscape. They are different both in kind

Bletchley Park. (JH)

and in number from the hundred or more we have so far met. For these were men and women shrouded in secrecy when World War II was raging and its outcome was far from certain. From a modest two hundred in 1939 their numbers reached some twelve thousand by the middle of 1945. They were the Code Breakers of Bletchley Park.

❖ ❖ ❖ ❖ ❖

Bletchley Park is a Victorian manson set in some fifty-five acres. but it has a history dating back across the centuries to the time of the Conquest. Indeed, though Bletchley Park has not been named as such in the preceding chapters of this book, it has nevertheless been connected with many of the historic figures we have so far considered. Geoffrey of Coutances, the Giffards, the de Greys, the Villiers, Thomas Willis and Browne Willis . . . all these were historic figures in the centuries from the 11th to the 18th. They owned, and lost, the Manor of Whaddon in the Bletchley area. By 1711 the then Lord of the Manor, Browne Willis, built a new Manor House called Water Hall. He never lived in it, but died in its predecessor, Whaddon Hall, in 1760. By 1798 Water Hall was sold and was pulled down by its new owner. The estate changed hands more than once and was finally bought in 1883 by Herbert Leon, Liberal MP for North Bucks. Leon gradually enlarged the Victorian mansion and developed its parkland. He was in effect the Lord of the Manor of what remained from the Manor of Whaddon which had existed through many vicissitudes for the past eight hundred years.

Sir Herbert Leon died in 1926 and his widow, Lady Leon, died in 1937. The Bletchley Park Estate was then put on the market. The expectation was that the estate would be split into smaller areas for residential development and that the mansion itself would be demolished. However, this did not happen. By then war clouds were gathering and Government was looking for some quiet rural base in which to house its Code and Cypher School, a department of the Foreign Office.

A Small Beginning

By the summer of 1938 the Code and Cypher School began its work at Bletchley Park. In a quiet way it began its tasks of radio eavesdropping and code breaking. During the next five years the modest two hundred who began the programme swelled to some twelve thousand by 1945.

Before we consider their remarkable story we should take note of a parallel but separate programme which was also carried on. If Bletchley Park was concerned with the RECEPTION of German signals, other places in the vicinity were concerned with the OUTWARD transmission of British signals. For this Woburn Abbey was the secret headquarters. There, the Stable Wing and the Riding School were adapted for the purpose. The small hangar, once occupied by the aeroplane of the late Duchess of Bedford, became a type-composing room manned by compositors from the Oxford University Press. Propaganda leaflets typeset at Woburn were taken for printing to HM Stationery Office at Harrow.

Hugh Dalton, Minister of Economic Warfare, was head of the SOE (Special Operations Executive). Richard Crossman was for some time head of the German Department, assisted by his Secretary, High Gaitskill. So in those war years three men who later went on to high political office, Dalton, Crossman, and Gaitskill, found themselves on secret war work at Woburn.

Side by side with the production and dissemination of propaganda material, there was also broadcasting. For this Wavendon Tower and Whaddon Hall were used. Bogus radio stations operated also from Dawn Edge in Aspley Guise.

Sefton Delmer, operating from a secret house in Aspley Guise, set up two counterfeit radio stations. One purported to be Soldantensender Calais (Soldiers Radio Calais), and the other was operated as Deutscher Kurzwellen-sender (German Shortwave Radio Atlantic).

Another Propaganda station pretended to be a shortwave transmitter operating from behind the Eastern Front. In fact it operated from Paris House, in the grounds of Woburn Abbey.

❖ ❖ ❖ ❖ ❖

We return now to Bletchley Park itself and to the astonishing record of how men and women of genius covertly assembled there to master the secrets of the German Enigma Machine. Their success enabled the Allies to monitor the thousands of signals sent out daily by the German High Command to all units of their Navy, Army and Air Forces. Italian and Japanese Codes were also broken and read.

Bletchley Park, 'the best kept secret of World War II', may not have won the war single-handedly for the Allies, but assuredly it helped the Allies not to lose that war.

The Enigma Machine.

It shortened the conflict by anything up to two years and in doing so it saved the lives of countless thousands on both sides.

It is impossible to over-stress the importance of the work done at Bletchley Park by these truly historic figures in the Buckinghamshire landscape. They came quietly and settled in lodgings all over Bletchley and the surrounding areas. If asked what they did they replied that they were 'working for the Foreign Office'. That reply had to satisfy their landladies. The men and women in 'digs' were sometimes called Guinea Pigs, because their landladies were paid a guinea a week to house and feed them. They were a strange assortment of individuals . . . many of them men and women of genius. One of their number wrote the following anonymously:

BLETCHLEY PARK

To think that I should ever see
a sight so curious as BP;
a place called up at war's behest
and peopled with the queerly-dressed.
Yet what they did they could not say
Now ever shall till Judgment Day.

For 6 long years have we been there
subject to local scorn and stare.
We came by transport and by train,
the dull, the brilliantly insane;
What were we for? Where shall we be
when God at last redunds BP?

The Air Force types who never fly,
Soldiers who never do or die,
Land-lubber Sailors, beards complete,
Long-haired civilians, slim, effete.
Why they were there they never knew
And what they told you wasn't true.

If I should die, think this of me
I served my country at BP.
And should my son ask: 'What did you
in the Atomic World War do?'
God only knows . . . and He won't tell
for after all BP was Hell.

The Bletchley Park estate was surrounded by barbed wire and was guarded by units of the RAF Regiment. The no doubt apocryphal story is related that the airforce men were told by their officers to keep on their toes and were warned that if they failed to keep proper security they would themselves be sent 'inside the Park', leaving unspoken the notion that Bletchley Park was some kind of asylum!

Enigma

The dictionary definition of 'enigma' is: 'a person, thing, or situation that is mysterious, puzzling, or ambiguous'. Enigma is also the apt name the Germans gave to the ingenious machine they had developed for encoding and transmitting military signals. Throughout the 1930s they had refined and improved its efficiency to the point where they believed it to be impenetrable and unbreakable.

They were wrong. World War II began on September 3rd 1939. Only a few short weeks before that, in July 1939, Intelligence Officers of Poland, Britain and France met in secret in Pyry Forest in Poland. Polish Intelligence Officers there shared with their British and French counterparts the work they had been doing on monitoring the German Enigma signals. They were even able to hand over early copies of the Enigma machine itself.

This was the initial breakthrough the Intelligence Officers at Bletchley Park needed. The mastery of Enigma called for all the skill and ingenuity that scientists and mathematicians could bring to bear on it. The numbers of such scientific and mathematical geniuses assembled at Bletchley Park grew steadily from the modest nucleus who began the work in 1939. The Germans continued to modify their Engima machines all through the war. At Bletchley Park such modifications were an unending challenge, and the battle of wits was unrelenting.

The work went on round the clock. In three shifts each day the 'reading' of Enigma signals never ceased. And, despite the numbers of personnel involved at Bletchley Park (some twelve thousand by the war's end), the Germans never did learn that their impenetrable and unbreakable codes were being penetrated and broken in the heart of the Buckinghamshire countryside. To describe the Bletchley Park saga as 'Britain's best kept secret' is no idle boast.

To cope with the volume of work being done at Bletchley Park a large number of temporary buildings were erected alongside the original mansion. They were always referred to as Huts and were numbered. Hut 6 was the one where

Some of the solidly-built blocks erected in 1941–2.

Welchman and his cryptanalytical team first broke the Enigma Code. Navy cryptanalysis was focussed in Hut 8. Hut 3 was involved with both the Luftwaffe and the German Army.

In 1941 and 1942 a number of brick and concrete blocks were built. While the Huts were numbered, the blocks were identified by letters, A to G. They were heavily constructed and reinforced with massive concrete and steel girders, and they were designed to be gas-proof. In one such block the future Lord Jenkins worked. Roy Jenkins was then a young Army Captain. Of all the wartime buildings erected at the Park, the blocks remain today in excellent repair.

Colossus

Only many years after the war would it be revealed that the world's first-ever Computer was assembled at Bletchley Park. It was called 'Colossus'. The name is apt in more ways than one. It was huge – measuring 16 feet long, 12 feet deep, and 8 feet high. It used about 1,500 valves. The time would come after the

*Colossus, the
first computer.*

war when valves would be replaced by transistors, which in turn would make way for microchips, and we would all come to marvel at the astonishing miniaturisation of modern computers. Meanwhile nothing can detract from the genius of those who built 'Colossus' at Bletchley Park, the true ancestor of all computers.

The first Colossus could speed up the reading of electronic punched-tape to 5,000 characters a second. Ten other Colossi were added, each operating on 2,500 valves, and these could read up to 25,000 characters a second.

It is a remarkable fact that from first to last the Germans had no idea that the Enigma Machine was in allied hands and was being 'read' 24 hours a day. The Germans knew nothing of Bletchley Park or of what went on there. So BP never became a target for German bombs.

But on the night of November 30th, 1940, German bombs *did* fall on Bletchley Park. A single German bomber dropped six of them. One fell on Rickley Lane, a second on Elmers Park; the third and fourth bombs fell within the area of the Park itself. The fifth bomb fell in the adjacent Home Farm. The sixth bomb which also fell near Home Farm, did not explode, and was safely defused next day.

If those bombs had seriously damaged or destroyed Bletchley Park on that November night in 1940 the whole course of the war would have been dramatically, and perhaps disastrously, changed. It has been conjectured that the lone German bomber had become separated from a main German bombing raid heading for the Midlands. Or it may be that the bomber was intending to bomb the (then) important Wolverton Works a few miles away – or possible the Railway Loco Sheds and railyards of Bletchley Station just a few hundred yards from Bletchley Park. Either way, the six bombs did little damage and killed no-one.

Ultra

The name ULTRA covers the whole operation at Bletchley Park in the war years. In dictionary terms the word means 'beyond or surprising'. In the context of Intelligence a range of terms can be used: Secret, Most Secret, Top Secret. So unique and vital was the work done at Bletchley Park to crack the Enigma Machine and to read its thousands of signals, it was felt that a new classification of secrecy was needed for it. The word chosen was ULTRA, signifying a level and degree of secrecy far surpassing Secret, Most Secret, or Top Secret.

The Intelligence acquired through Ultra affected every aspect of the entire war against Germany, Italy and Japan. It embraced every phase of World War II, from the Battle of Britain to the final surrenders of the Axis powers. It covered the War in every ocean – Mediterranean, Atlantic, Pacific. And every continent – Europe, Asia, Africa.

So in the heart of the Buckinghamshire landscape history was made. And the twelve thousand who worked at Bletchley Park from 1939 to 1945 are truly historic figures in that landscape.

❖ ❖ ❖ ❖ ❖

When the War ended Bletchley Park ceased to be used by the Government Code and Cypher School and passed into the hands of the Civil Aviation Authority and, later, British Telecom. By early 1992 both of these bodies moved from Bletchley Park. There was a distinct possibility that Bletchley Park and its fifty-five acres would be treated as an area for development. The Milton Keynes Borough Council, however, declared most of Bletchley Park a Conservation Area.

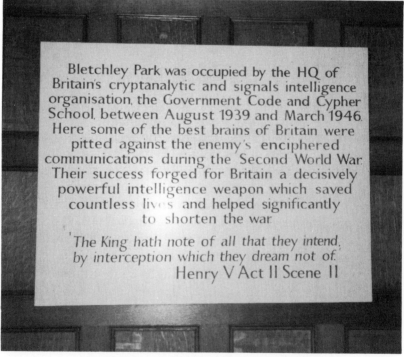

How prophetic Shakespeare's words were! (JH)

On February 13th 1992, the Bletchley Park Trust was set up with the aim of gaining recognition of the Park as a Heritage site and so saving it for the nation. By December 1993, the Trust opened offices in the Park and a programme was initiated to open the Park to the public at regular intervals. The Bletchley Park Trust has been registered as a Charity.

ALL ROYALTIES ON THIS BOOK WILL GO TO THE BLETCHLEY PARK TRUST, IN SALUTE TO ALL THOSE CODE BREAKERS WHO BETWEEN 1939 AND 1945 WERE SUCH ASTONISHING HISTORIC FIGURES IN THE BUCKINGHAMSHIRE LANDSCAPE.

Chapter 12

Bletchley Park Trust

Bletchley Park has two main claims to fame. Firstly there is the codebreaking work of 1939–45 which in all probability saved us from losing the war, and secondly the world's first electronic computers were built and operated there in 1943–45 as part of the codebreaking work.

The aim of the Trust is to save Bletchley Park for the nation. It was founded under rather dramatic circumstances in 1991 and registered as a charity in 1992.

The wartime work in breaking many of the Axis codes is now better known that it was when the Trust began. The secrecy in which the entire operation was wrapped was understandable during the war and although some details were released under the thirty year rule in the 1970s, the greater part of the information has become available only fifty years after the events in question. Even now, much is still unavailable.

During the War, the codebreakers were hampered in their efforts by their inability to explain precisely why they needed extra typists, and so on 21st October 1941, four of the principal officers involved wrote a letter to Mr Churchill explaining their predicament. October 21st is the anniversary of Trafalgar and the significance would not have been lost on the Prime Minister, who made one of his celebrated *Action this day* notes. Typists and other staff were promptly sent to Bletchley, thus increasing the flow of information to help the armed services.

At the instigation of the Bletchley Archaeological and Historical Society, a reunion of the codebreakers was held in Bletchley Park in 1991 to commemorate the letter of 1941. Many

Decryption of Enigma in Hut 6. It took intervention by Churchill to get enough typists for the round-the-clock work.

of the people who had been in the Park during the War were able for the first time to see an example of the Enigma machine whose messages they had decrypted so long before.

In 1991 the Park was on the point of closure and it was planned to demolish the wartime buildings in favour of a hypermarket and a housing estate. The codebreakers thought this to be inappropriate and a letter was composed to the Prime Minister asking that the Park should be saved; it was taken to Downing Street by a deputation which included Sir Stuart Milner-Barry, who had signed the original letter in 1941.

After this the Trust was set up and the Milton Keynes Borough Council made the Park a Conservation Area. the landowners – the Government and British Telecom – let some of the buildings to the Trust and the great enthusiasm for the Park brought in many allied groups so gradually exhibitions have been assembled and put on show. In the mansion is a remarkable collection of Churchilliana. Elsewhere are displays of military vehicles from jeeps to tanks, of fire engines, model boats (in summer we sail models on the lake), railways (with working models) and even a museum of the toys of the period.

There is a cinema projector collection, which shows wartime films, an aircraft recovery group, the Diplomatic Wireless Service museum, a collection of wartime uniforms, German and American re-enactment groups, galleries of radar equipment and computers – we believe we have the second oldest workable computer in Britain – examples of the clandestine radio sets sent to the Resistance during the war, and the Cryptology Trail, with examples of the Enigma, Lorenz, Geheimschreiber and Type X machines. Here you can see how messages were sent, intercepted by the Y service, sent back to Bletchley, decrypted and acted upon. Lastly there is the Colossus computer, rebuilt from original parts and in working order.

Other projects include the construction of a Post Office of the time – you can buy stamps there! – and the Bombe machine for breaking the key settings of the Enigma machine. New displays are constantly being installed. There is a lot to see and you should allow a minimum of three hours: many people come again and again.

Wrens adjusting Colossus, the world's first computer.

Bletchley Park has a pleasant ambience with a lake, lawns and a collection of specimen trees planted a century ago. Surprisingly little has altered in the last fifty years and with the uniformed members of the Trust marching about, you could easily think you had entered a time-warp of fifty years.

There is a fair range of wild life. During the summer there is a varied programme of special events such as model or military vehicle rallies.

At present Bletchley Park is open in alternate weekends, both Saturday and Sundays from 1030 to 1700 (5pm). There are guided tours on the hour every hour from 1100 to 1500 (3pm) and there are eating houses on the campus.

For further details of Open Days and of membership of the Friends of Bletchley Park please contact:

> The Bletchley Park Trust,
> Bletchley Park,
> Bletchley,
> MILTON KEYNES   MK3 6EF
>
> Telephone: 01908 640404
> Fax: 01908 274381

We think Bletchley Park is a site of outstanding national and international importance. We have plans, when we acquire the site, for national museums of telecommunications and computers, a conference centre and a hotel, set in the atmosphere of the period. We should like to restore the Victorian gardens to their former glory.

We look forward to seeing you at Bletchley Park.

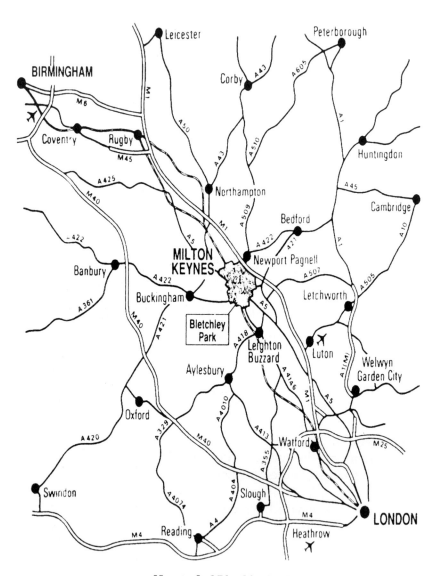

How to find Bletchley Park

Welcome to Bletchley Park

Britain's Best Kept Secret

You can see:

In Faulkner House
* Aircraft Recovery
* American Army
  Re-enactment
* Cinema Projectors
* Colossus Rebuild
* Computer Exhibition
* Cryptology Trail
* Diplomatic Wireless
* Home Front
* Radar & Electronics
* The Shop
* Uniforms

In Hut 11a
* Model Railways

In the garages
* Fire Engines
* Model Boats

The Cafe
* Park Tours start here

In the Mansion
* Churchill Collection
* Mansion Guided Tours
* Toy Collection

In the Motor Pool
* Military Vehicles

Main Entrance

Car Parks

Hut 4

The Huts 3, 6 & 8
wooden Huts
The second phase of

A & B Block
Naval intelligence

C Block
The enormous punched
card index of information

E Block
Japanese code breaking

D Block
Extension of Hut 3, 6 & 8
work

G Block
Traffic analysis and
deception operations

The Wartime Buildings

Bletchley Park ground plan.

INDEX

Books Published by
THE BOOK CASTLE

JOURNEYS INTO BEDFORDSHIRE: Anthony Mackay.
Foreword by The Marquess of Tavistock, Woburn Abbey.
A lavish book of over 150 evocative ink drawings.

A PILGRIMAGE IN HERTFORDSHIRE: H. M. Alderman.
Classic, between-the-wars tour round the county, embellished
with line drawings.

**COUNTRYSIDE CYCLING IN BEDFORDSHIRE,
Buckinghamshire and Hertfordshire**: Mick Payne.
Twenty rides on- and off-road for all the family.

**PUB WALKS FROM COUNTRY STATIONS:
Bedfordshire and Hertfordshire**: Clive Higgs.
Fourteen circular country rambles, each starting and finishing
at a railway station and incorporating a pub-stop at a mid-way
point.

LOCAL WALKS: South Bedfordshire and North Chilterns:
Vaughan Basham. Twenty-seven thematic circular walks.

LOCAL WALKS: North and Mid-Bedfordshire:
Vaughan Basham. Twenty-five thematic circular walks.

FAMILY WALKS: Chilterns South: Nick Moon.
Thirty 3 to 5 mile circular walks.

**CHILTERN WALKS: Hertfordshire, Bedfordshire and
North Buckinghamshire**: Nick Moon.
CHILTERN WALKS: Buckinghamshire: Nick Moon.
**CHILTERN WALKS: Oxfordshire and
West Buckinghamshire**: Nick Moon.
A trilogy of circular walks, in association with the Chiltern
Society. Each volume contains thirty circular walks.

**OXFORDSHIRE WALKS:
Oxford, the Cotswolds and the Cherwell Valley**: Nick Moon.
**OXFORDSHIRE WALKS:
Oxford, the Downs and the Thames Valley**: Nick Moon.
Two volumes that complement Chiltern Walks: Oxfordshire
and complete coverage of the county, in association with the
Oxford Fieldpaths Society. Thirty circular walks in each.

FOLK: Characters and Events in the History of Bedfordshire and Northamptonshire: Vivienne Evans.
Anthology about people of yesteryear – arranged alphabetically by village or town.

**LEGACIES:
Tales and Legends of Bedfordshire and Hertfordshire:**
Vic Lea. Twenty-five mysteries and stories based on fact, including Luton Town Football Club. Many photographs.

HISTORIC FIGURES IN THE BUCKINGHAMSHIRE LANDSCAPE: John Houghton.
Major personalities and events that have shaped the county's past, including a special section on Bletchley Park.

**MANORS and MAYHEM, PAUPERS and POLITICS:
Tales from Four Shires: Beds., Bucks., Herts., and Northants.**: John Houghton.
Little-known historical snippets and stories.

**MYTHS and WITCHES, PEOPLE and POLITICS:
Tales from Four Shires: Bucks., Beds., Herts., and Northants.**: John Houghton.
Anthology of strange but true historical events.

**ECCENTRICS and VILLAINS, HAUNTINGS and HEROES:
Tales from Four Shires: Northants., Beds., Bucks., and Herts.**: John Houghton.
True incidents and curious events covering one thousand years.

DUNSTABLE WITH THE PRIORY, 1100–1550: Vivienne Evans.
Dramatic growth of Henry I's important new town around a major crossroads.

**DUNSTABLE DECADE: THE EIGHTIES:
A Collection of Photographs**: Pat Lovering.
A souvenir book of nearly 300 pictures of people and events in the 1980s.

DUNSTABLE IN DETAIL: Nigel Benson.
A hundred of the town's buildings and features, plus town trail map.

OLD DUNSTABLE: Bill Twaddle.
A new edition of this collection of early photographs.

THE RAILWAY AGE IN BEDFORDSHIRE: Fred Cockman.
Classic, illustrated acount of early railway history.

CHILTERN ARCHAEOLOGY: RECENT WORK:
A Handbook for the Next Decade: edited by Robin Holgate.
The latest views, results and excavations by twenty-three leading archaeologists throughout the Chilterns.

WHIPSNADE WILD ANIMAL PARK: 'MY AFRICA': Lucy Pendar.
Foreword by Andrew Forbes. Introduction by Gerald Durrell.
Inside story of sixty years of the Park's animals and people – full of anecdotes, photographs and drawings.

BOURNE and BRED:
A Dunstable Boyhood Between the Wars: Colin Bourne.
An elegantly written, well-illustrated book capturing the spirit of the town over fifty years ago.

ROYAL HOUGHTON: Pat Lovering.
Illustrated history of Houghton Regis from the earliest times to the present.

BEDFORDSHIRE'S YESTERYEARS Vol. 1:
The Family, Childhood and Schooldays:
Brenda Fraser-Newstead.
Unusual early 20th century reminiscences, with private photographs.

BEDFORDSHIRE'S YESTERYEARS Vol. 2:
The Rural Scene: Brenda Fraser-Newstead.
Vivid first-hand accounts of country life two or three generations ago.

BEDFORDSHIRE'S YESTERYEARS Vol. 3:
Craftsmen and Trades People:
Brenda Fraser-Newstead.
Fascinating recollections over several generations practising many vanishing crafts and trades.

BEDFORDSHIRE'S YESTERYEARS Vol. 4:
War Times and Civil Matters:
Brenda Fraser-Newstead.
Two World Wars, plus transport, law and order, etc.

THE CHANGING FACE OF LUTON: An Illustrated History:
Stephen Bunker, Robin Holgate and Marian Nichols.
Luton's development from earliest times to the present busy industrial town. Illustrated in colour and monochrome. The three authors from Luton Museum are all experts in local history, archaeology, crafts and social history.

THE MEN WHO WORE STRAW HELMETS:
Policing Luton, 1840–1974: Tom Madigan.
Meticulously chronicled history; dozens of rare photographs; author served in Luton Police for nearly fifty years.

BETWEEN THE HILLS:
The Story of Lilley, a Chiltern Village: Roy Pinnock.
A priceless piece of our heritage – the rural beauty remains but the customs and way of life described here have largely disappeared.

GLEANINGS REVISITED:
Nostalgic Thoughts of a Bedfordshire's Farmer's Boy:
E W O'Dell.
His own sketches and early photographs adorn this lively account of rural Bedfordshire in days gone by.

FARM OF MY CHILDHOOD, 1925–1947: Mary Roberts.
An almost vanished lifestyle on a remote farm near Flitwick.

THE VALE OF THE NIGHTINGALE:
The True Story of a Harpenden Family: Molly Andrews.
Victorian times to the present day in this lovely village.

THE TALL HITCHIN SERGEANT:
A Victorian Crime Novel based on fact:
Edgar Newman.
Mixes real police officers and authentic background with an exciting storyline.

THE TALL HITCHIN INSPECTOR'S CASEBOOK:
A Victorian Crime Novel based on fact:
Edgar Newman.
Worthies of the time encounter more archetypal villains.

LEAFING THROUGH LITERATURE: Writer's Lives
in Hertfordshire and Bedfordshire:
David Carroll.
Illustrated short biographies of many famous authors and their connections with these counties.

THE HILL OF THE MARTYR: An Architectural History
of St. Albans Abbey: Eileen Roberts.
Scholarly and readable chronological narrative history of Hertfordshire and Bedfordshire's famous cathedral. Fully illustrated with photographs and plans.

SPECIALLY FOR CHILDREN

VILLA BELOW THE KNOLLS:
A Story of Roman Britain:
Michael Dundrow.
An exciting adventure for young John in Totternhoe and Dunstable two thousand years ago.

ADVENTURE ON THE KNOLLS:
A Story of Iron Age Britain:
Michael Dundrow.
Excitement on Totternhoe Knolls as ten-year-old John finds himself back in those dangerous times, confronting Julius Caesar and his army.

THE RAVENS:
One Boy Against the Might of Rome:
James Dyer.
On the Barton Hills and in the south-east of England as the men of the great fort of Ravensburgh (near Hexton) confront the invaders.

Further titles are in preparation.
All the above are available via any bookshop, or from the publisher and bookseller

THE BOOK CASTLE
12 Church Street, Dunstable Bedfordshire, LU5 4RU
Tel: (01582) 605670